RUSSIA

UNDER THE TZARS.

BY

S. STEPNIAK,

AUTHOR OF "UNDERGROUND RUSSIA.'

Translated by

WILLIAM WESTALL,

AUTHOR OF "RED RYVINGTON," ETC.

IN TWO VOLUMES.

VOL. I.

London:

WARD AND DOWNEY,

12, YORK STREET, COVENT GARDEN.

1885.

PREFACE.

Russia is passing through a crisis of great importance in her social and political life. Within a brief space of time the revolutionary movement has attained a marvellous growth, and is spreading more and more among the classes which have heretofore been the chief supporters of the established order. The very ferocity of a reaction bewildered by personal fear is dragging it to its inevitable doom, and, like the French usurper of December 2nd, the morally ruined Government of the Tzar is meditating that most desperate of all expedients for the restoration of vanished prestige—a bloody and useless war.

The growing disquietude of the masses, manifested in wild outbursts against the Jews, and in less irrational, though hardly less frequent, riots and disturbances, as well in agricultural districts as in manufacturing centres—whether as protests against

exacting landlords, tyrannical masters, or oppressive
laws for the regulation of factory labour, are facts
that cannot be gainsaid, and the significance of which
it is impossible to overlook. They show what everybody feels in his heart, if he does not speak it aloud—
that momentous changes are pending, and that Russia
is on the eve of great events.

None would be so rash as to attempt to forecast the
nature of these events or guess what the fates may
have in store for the empire of the Tzar. But of one
thing there can be no question : revolutionary changes
cannot take place in a country so vast, and whose
population is a third of that of all Europe, without
affecting, directly or indirectly, every other country of
the civilized world.

This fact is the justification and explanation of the
growing interest that is everywhere felt in Russia
and her people, and in the hidden forces which are
working out her destinies and shaping her future.

Many valuable contributions have been made on
the subject to the literature of the day by foreign
writers—French, English, and German. But hitherto
the European public have seldom, if ever, heard the
views of those who, being the most interested in the
question, are naturally the most competent to give an
opinion—the Russians themselves.

Russian writers, among whom are many able men

of honourable name and great erudition, remain silent; they do not raise their voices to tell the truth about their oppressed country. The cause of this strange silence is easy of explanation. It were as perilous an undertaking for a subject of the Tzar to reveal to the outside world the iniquities of his Government as openly to attack him in the presence of his police. Except a few anonymous articles of slight importance, our best writers have, as yet, said nothing on the politics of Russia in the languages of Europe. The Government party alone and their allies have been able to turn to account the publicity of the Press; but their contributions to the question, it is hardly necessary to say, do not tend to the enlightenment of public opinion.

In these circumstances the task of speaking for the opposite party—that is to say, for the whole of educated Russia—falls naturally to the extreme fraction of the opposition—revolutionists, Socialists, and refugees of every class—who from time to time have tried to win the ear of Europe. And now this duty falls on me—a "Nihilist writer," a "practical Nihilist," as some English newspapers have been good enough to call me—a man whose sole claim to the indulgence of the English public is the authorship of a book having for its object the explanation and defence of Nihilism—a claim which is far from being the most efficient for

such a work as mine. I would willingly have left the
task to the member of a less advanced school, who
might be less open than myself to the charge of
a too great pessimism in his appreciation of the
existing system. But there being no such writer at
hand, I have no alternative. The work must be
done by me ; and whatever other merits or demerits
my book may possess, it has at least been done impartially.

Knowing beforehand the points as to which my
readers are likely to be most distrustful, I resolved
above all things to avoid exaggeration, and I have
aimed throughout at saying too little rather than too
much. In this there is no difficulty, for the wrongs
done by the Russian Government are so immeasurable
that they may be attenuated with no more seeming
effect than is made on the fathomless ocean by taking
from it a glass of water; whilst, on the other hand, a
slight overstatement on a comparatively immaterial
point might impair the value, if not render abortive,
months of careful and conscientious labour. Yet I
neither intend nor desire to put the existing
régime in any better light than it deserves. Not at
all. Though I " nothing set down in malice," I
" nothing extenuate." I tell only the plain, un-
varnished truth, but it is the full truth. In the
selection of my facts I have taken the greatest care,

rejecting everything that seemed without warrant or not altogether trustworthy.

I have not swollen the dimensions of my book with unnecessary references and notes. The things I have told may be new to foreigners, but to Russians and to all who know Russian literature they are matters of common knowledge.

In my historical sketches I have availed myself of the works of our best historical writers (Kostomaroff, Solovieff, Serguevitch, and Belaeff), works which are to be found in every Russian library. The matters set forth in the second volume are taken from official sources, and from statements which have been allowed to appear in the censured Press at times when it has enjoyed brief snatches of unwonted freedom.

The six chapters of the second volume have appeared at various times in the most influential of English papers, and I have to thank the *Times* for its eloquent and appreciative comments on my communications, and the proprietors for the kind permission to include them in the book. All the rest of the two volumes is original.

It is evident that, as touching the first part of the book, I could not avail myself to any great extent of official publications or newspaper statements. The cruelties inflicted on prisoners and the iniquities of the administration can seldom be openly mentioned in the censured Press, and then only in guarded and evasive language. The excellent publications of the _Narodnia Volia_ printing-office at Geneva, which are as carefully compiled and as trustworthy as they are rich in material have been my chief sources of information. Many of my statements are drawn either from my own personal experience or from the experience of friends who have been good enough to place them at my disposal. I have merely put their narratives into literary shape.

A word as to the form of my book. It is irregular and not strictly didactic, for I have tried not alone to narrate events but to describe men. Critics will perhaps say that this double aim derogates from the dignity of a serious work. They may be right. I will only observe that on this point moderation and sobriety have been my rule.

These explanations rendered, there remains for me only one more duty to perform—the agreeable duty of thanking those who have given me their aid in the writing of my book.

Being as yet new in the country, and unable to write the English language with ease, I am indebted to Mr. William Westall, who has long been a warm sympathizer with the Russian revolutionary cause, and my literary fellow-worker, for giving the work its English shape; and I heartily thank him for his careful and idiomatic translation.

As for the matter of the book, I owe many thanks to some of my countrymen. Mr. Peter Lavroff, to whom I am indebted for the very kind Introduction to my "Underground Russia," which so greatly contributed to the success of my first work, has been good enough to place his rich library at my disposal for the preparation of "Russia Under the Tzars," my second work. To Mr. Isidor Goldsmith, formerly editor of *Znanie* and *Slovo*, Mr. Nicolas Tsakny, and Mr. L. N., all of whom have spent years in exile, I am obliged for much of the interesting information which I have utilized in the chapters on that subject.

But most of all I have to thank Mr. Michel Dragomanoff, formerly one of the professors at Kieff University, who, from the very beginning of my campaign against the Russian despotism—first in the pages of the *Contemporary Review*, and afterwards in the columns of the *Times*—has given me, without stint of time or trouble, much valuable assistance, and in connection with the present work has supplied me with many original and authentic documents relating to police persecution in the three satrapies of the South.

S. STEPNIAK.

LONDON,
April 7, 1885.

CONTENTS.

PART I.

THE EVOLUTION OF THE AUTOCRACY.

PART III.

ADMINISTRATIVE EXILE.

village mayor), recognizing as valid only such meetings as he might convene, and making his own
election contingent on the approval of the so-called
mediator, a high functionary appointed jointly by the
Government and the local nobility. In the original
state, however—that is to say, where the administration has not been strong enough to enforce the
measures it proposed—the communal autonomy has
suffered no restriction.

The *mir* of Central Russia—in Southern Russia
the *gromada*—is the peasant's conception of supreme
authority; it safeguards the welfare of the entire
community, and is entitled to the implicit obedience
of every individual of whom it is composed. It may
be convened by its humblest member at any time and
at any place within the limits of the village. The
communal authorities must respond respectfully to
the summons, and, if they fail in their duty, the
assembly may dismiss them from their offices without
notice, or deprive them for an indefinite period of all
their authority.

The meetings of a village commune, like those of
the Landesgemeinde of the primitive Swiss cantons,
are held under the vault of heaven, before the *starosta's* house, before a tavern, or at any other convenient place. The thing that most strikes a person
who is present for the first time at one of these

meetings is the utter confusion which seem to cha-
racterize its proceedings. Chairman there is none;
the debates are scenes of the wildest disorder.
After the convener has explained his reasons for
calling the meeting, everybody rushes in to express
his opinion, and for a while the debate resembles a
free fight of pugilists. The right of speaking belongs
to him who can command attention. If an orator
pleases his audience, interrupters are promptly
silenced; but if he says nothing worth hearing,
nobody heeds him, and he is " shut up " by the first
opponent. When the question is somewhat of a
burning one, and the meeting begins to grow warm,
all speak at once, and none listen. On these occasions the assembly breaks up into groups, each of
which discusses the subject on its own account.
Everybody shouts his arguments at the top of his
voice; shrieks and objurgations, words of contumely
and derision are heard on every hand, and a wild
uproar goes on, from which it does not seem possible
that any good can result.

But this apparent confusion is of no moment. It
is a necessary means to a certain end. In our village
assemblies voting is unknown; controversies are never
decided by a majority of voices. Every question must
be settled unanimously. Hence the general debate, as
well as private discussions, have to be continued until

a proposal is brought forward which conciliates all interests and wins the suffrage of the entire *mir*. It is, moreover, evident that to reach this consummation the debates must be thorough and the subject well threshed out ; and, in order to overcome isolated opposition, it is essential for the advocates of conflicting views to be brought face to face, and compelled to fight out their differences in single combat.

The method of adjustment I have described is eminently characteristic of the Russian *mir*. The assembly does not force on the minority resolutions with which the latter is unable to agree. Everybody must make concessions for the general good and the peace and welfare of the community. The majority are too generous to take advantage of their numerical strength. The *mir* is not a master, but a loving parent, equally compassionate to all its children. It is this quality of our village self-government that explains the high sense of humanity which forms so marked a feature of our rural customs—the mutual help in field labour, the aid given to the poor, the fatherless, and the afflicted—which have elicited the warm admiration of every observer of our village life. To the same cause must be ascribed the unswerving loyalty of Russian peasants to their *mir*. "Whatever the *mir* decides is ordained of God," says a popular proverb. There are many other sayings as, for

instance: "Nobody but God dare judge the *mir*;"
"Who is greater than the *mir*? who can dispute with
it?" "The *mir* receives no bribes;" "Where the
mir's hand is, there my head is;" "Although last
in the *mir*, a man is always one of the flock; but
once separated from the *mir*, he is but an orphan;"
"Every member of the *mir* is as a member of the
same family."

An indispensable corollary to the integrity of the
mir, and, seeing how the country is ruled, one of its
most surprising peculiarities, is the full liberty of
speech and debate enjoyed by our rural assemblies.
Indispensable, for how could business be done and
justice enforced if, instead of speaking their minds
freely, members of a commune were to fear giving
offence to Peter or John, and resort to subterfuge and
falsehood? Rough frankness of manner and unre-
strained liberty of speech being adopted as a rule and
sanctioned by tradition, they are not abandoned when
by chance there comes under discussion some subject
outside the modest sphere of peasant life. It is a
fact admitted by all observers that, while in the cities
words implying "disrespect of existing institutions"
are uttered even in private with bated breath and
heard with trembling, the peasants in their public
meetings talk as they list, criticise the very institu-
tutions which others are permitted only to admire,

censure with easy impartiality the most illustrious members of the administrative oligarchy, treat boldly the burning agrarian question, and often express opinions concerning the sacred imperial presence itself which would make the hair of a well-bred townsman stand on end.

It must not, however, be supposed that this license of language bespeaks an insubordinate temper or a rebellious spirit. It is nothing more than an inveterate habit begotten of long usage. The peasants have no idea that in speaking their minds they are breaking the law. They do not understand how speech, opinion—whatever the method of its expression—can be considered a crime. There are cases on record of a *starosta* receiving revolutionary proclamations by post and, in the innocence of his heart, reading them aloud before the village assembly as something curious and suggestive. If a revolutionary propagandist happens to enter a village he is invited to meet the assembly and read or tell whatever he may think likely to edify the community. What harm could arise from so natural a proceeding? And if the fact becomes known nothing can exceed the surprise of the peasants when told by the gendarmes that they have committed a heinous offence. So great is their ignorance that they believe liberty of speech to be a right inherent in every rational being !

Such are the main features of our village self-government. Nothing can well be more striking than the contrast between the institutions which prevail among the lower orders of Russia and the institutions which regulate the lives of its upper classes. The former are essentially republican and democratic; the latter are based on imperial despotism, and organized on the strictest principles of bureaucratic control.

This contrast, so palpable and portentous, having endured for centuries, has produced, as its inevitable consequence, a phenomenon of great importance—that strongly marked tendency of the Russian people to hold themselves aloof from the State, which is one of their most significant characteristics. On the one hand, the peasant saw before him his *mir*, the embodiment of justice and brotherly love; on the other, official Russia, represented by the *tchinovniks* of the Tzar, his magistrates, gendarmes, and administrators — through all the centuries of our history the embodiment of rapacity, venality, and violence. In these circumstances it was not difficult to make a choice. "It is better," says the peasant of to-day, "to stand guilty before the *mir* than innocent before the judge." And his forefathers said, "Live and enjoy yourselves, children, while Moscow takes no notice of you."

From the very dawn of our national history the

Russian peasant has shunned intercourse with the Russia of the *tchinovniks*. The two have never mingled, a fact which explains why the political evolutions of ages have made so little impression on the habits of our toiling millions. It is no exaggeration to say that the lives of the bulk of the nation and of its upper classes have flowed in two contiguous yet separate and distinct streams. The common folks live in their liliputian republics like snails in their shells. To them official Russia—the world of *tchinovniks*, soldiers, and policemen—is a horde of foreign conquerors, who from time to time send their agents into the country to demand the tribute of money and the tribute of blood—taxes for the Tzar's treasury and soldiers for his army. Yet by a startling anomaly—one of those strange contrasts of which, as a celebrated geographer has said, Russia is full—these rudimentary republics, which enjoy so large a measure of social and personal freedom, are at once the surest foundations and the strongest bulwarks of despotic power.

By what vagary of fortune or caprice of history, it may be asked, has this crying anomaly arisen? How comes it that institutions in so flagrant contradiction with the whole of our political *régime* as these peasant parliaments should flourish under the ægis of an arbitrary monarch?

The anomaly is only in appearance; we have to deal neither with an historical riddle nor the fortuitous results of incidental combinations. I lay so much stress on our system of popular self-government because I am convinced that the form which it takes and ideas whereon it is based are more in conformity with the political aspirations of the Russian people than the autocratic and centralized form of the existing system. If there be aught anomalous in our polity, aught imposed on the nation by outward and accidental causes, it is the despotism itself.

CHAPTER II.

THE VETCHE.

At the beginning of authentic history the vast country now known as Russia was divided into a number of principalities varying in extent, having each a capital and several more or less important towns and villages. The rulers, however, were not supreme; they reigned but they did not govern, all legislative and executive power being vested in the popular assembly. This assembly was composed of free citizens without distinction of rank or fortune, the prince being no more than a public functionary, elected by the people and obedient to their will. By traditional custom the princes were chosen among the members of the same family from generation to generation, or, rather, from a race of warriors of royal blood, all of whom claimed descent from Rurik, the supposed founder of the Russian Empire. The principle of heredity was not, however, regarded

as an immutable law; the *vetche* recognized no such
right, and when a native prince was not to the taste
of his people, they changed him for one more to
their liking. The prince was subject, not superior to
his people; the subjection of the people being an
idea which did not come into vogue until several
centuries later. The privilege was however seldom
exercised. Russian history contains, but few instances of the deposition of a native prince in favour
of a foreign ruler; and once only, when the people
of Galitia deemed a change expedient, was a simple
boyard raised to princely rank. But the custom
of choosing rulers from the same family was really
no restriction on the liberty of election; for the
royal stock so increased and multiplied, and established so many off-shoqts in different parts of the
country, that suitable candidates were always forthcoming.

Some historians of the so-called Muscovite school,
out of pure love for monarchic principles, have pretended to discover the germ of this form of government
in the supposed laws of succession and right of birth
among the princes of ancient Russia. But the more
thorough and impartial researches of the new school
prove that no such laws existed, that no such rights
were recognized—the relations between the reigning
prince and the people being in every case regulated

by the *vetche*. The nearest of kin to the ruler had
naturally the best opportunities of making himself
favourably known ; and in ancient Russia, as among
all patriarchal nations, age commanded popular
respect. When a prince died or was banished
the ruler generally chosen to succeed him was his
eldest brother, who was probably also the head of
the family, or of that branch of it which the people
delighted to honour. If, however, the brother were
unpopular, he would be passed over, the choice in
that event falling on the son of the late prince ; or,
again, if the people so willed it, the uncle and the
nephew might both be superseded by a prince whose
kinship to the royal line was attenuated almost past
recognition ; for mere genealogy counted for nothing
in the matter, and early Russian history affords
abundant evidence that the one immutable privilege
which regulated the succession was the will of the
vetche.

The call of a prince was, however, only the first
step in his election. The next proceeding was the
conclusion of a convention—the *riada*—between the
new ruler and the city. Both parties swore faithfully
to observe the contract, and without the *riada* no
prince could consider his position safe. The *riada*,
in fact, was the constitutional pact. It defined the
mutual obligations of the contracting parties. The

conditions of the compact were subject to modifica-
tions, not only in different principalities and from
time to time, but as between one prince and
another. The leading conditions of the pact were
nevertheless almost always identical. The highest
function of the prince was that of judge. In the
smaller principalities he alone filled this office, and
in many of the contracts it was specially stipulated
that the prince should act in person, never by deputy,
the people having more confidence in the impartiality
and independence of their prince than in any of his
men. At a later period, when princes, influenced by
other ideas, began to trespass on the popular rights,
it was specified in the constitutional pacts that the
prince should only act as judge when assisted by a
colleague appointed by the *vetche.*

A second duty of the prince, hardly less important
than the first, was to defend the country from its
enemies ; but the right to declare war, or to dispose
of the military forces which were composed of all
citizens able to bear arms, was vested in the *vetche.*
The prince, generally a man trained to arms from his
youth upwards, was appointed to the command of the
army only after the declaration of war, and in the
more important principalities he shared the responsi-
bilities of command with a special officer elected by
the *vetche.* The prince had always in his service a

more or less numerous corps of volunteers—free fighters—half of them native, and half foreign, denominated *drugina,* or "friends of the prince." And so they were—literally his friends—meeting every day in the same hall, sitting at the same table, the companions of all his amusements, his advisers in every difficulty. They were, moreover, maintained entirely at his expense, either out of the revenues granted to him by the *vetche* or his own private resources. If he desired to make war, the *vetche* was at liberty to refuse him the co-operation of the militia. In this event he could, however, undertake it at his own risk and peril, with the help of his *drugina,* a privilege of which the princes of that age often availed themselves to their great advantage. The *drugina,* being the prince's personal companions, followed him everywhere. If he left his principality to rule over a richer and larger community, they accompanied him and shared his good fortune. On the other hand, when the citizens dismissed an un-popular ruler, the *drugina* were expelled at the same time.

Changes like these were of frequent occurrence, and there were few princes who had not occupied in the course of their lives half-a-dozen thrones (or "dinner tables," according to the suggestive phrase then in vogue). A change of rulers was easily effected. When a prince became unpopular, the *vetche* had simply to meet and pronounce the sacramental phrase, "We salute thee, O Prince!" whereupon his Highness would retire, feeling no more ill-will for his former constituents than if he were a candidate for parliamentary honours beaten at an election. If his successor did not prove a success, and the *vetche* again changed their minds and recalled him, he would resume his former position with the greatest alacrity. It sometimes came to pass that a prince was elected, dismissed, and re-elected three or four times in succession by the very same city.

Thus the principalities of mediæval Russia, notwithstanding the monarchical form of their government, were in reality so many free republics, and republics they are called by the best of our modern historians, Mr. Kostomaroff, although with a delicate consideration for the susceptibilities of the censorship, he avoids the use of the Latin term, substituting for it the Slav equivalent *narodopravstvo*. The princes were practically soldiers of fortune, with a following of volunteers whom the republics took into their service. A state of things not very dissimilar prevailed in the small Italian republics of the Middle Ages, the sole difference being that the Russian *condottieri* formed a separate caste and were all descended from the same royal stock.

Yet this, difference was far from being detrimental to the democratic institutions of the period, for the most striking fact in our early history is the entire absence of any tendencies towards tyranny. Rarely, indeed, do we find a prince opposing by force the popular will. There was too much to lose thereby and too little to gain. A people half nomad, living in a country so thinly inhabited that the land had no value, could have no strong local ties. Neither did the prince's love of country count for much. As nomadic as the people themselves, he and his *drugina* cared not whither they went nor where they settled. Every prince for himself, and the *drugina* for their master, were always on the look-out for promotion; that is to say, for a larger city and better pay. It was therefore against a prince's own interest to resist the will of the *vetche*, for such a stain on his reputation would greatly impair his chances of advancement. In default of anything better, moreover, he could always find some petty principality ready to receive him, for a town governed by a simple *posadnik* always added to its distinction and independence by exchanging his rule for that of a prince. In the meantime he might look forward with confidence to something better. Princes were so often dethroned and conflicts with the *vetche* were so common that a royal adventurer with a good character who kept his eyes open had little difficulty in obtaining the promotion to which he aspired. At the worst, it was always possible for a prince of enterprise to win honour and wealth by force of arms at the expense of his less warlike kinsmen. In these conquests there was nothing tyrannical or hostile to liberty. A popular prince ran little risk of attack; for would-be aggressors knew that they would have to deal not with the *drugina* alone, but the entire military force of the country. On the other hand, when the people had no particular love for their prince it was a matter of indifference to them whether he won or lost. In the latter event they were quite ready to accept as ruler the prince who had proved himself the better man. The *vetche* elected the victor, who immediately signed the *riada*, and, after taking the usual oath, entered on his functions precisely as if he had acquired his position in the ordinary way. If he in his turn made himself unpopular, there was a simple and infallible way of getting rid of him. The *vetche* had only to offer the throne on more than usually favourable terms to some prince of military capacity, whereupon the latter would appear on the scene with his *drugina*, and, aided by the citizens, depose his rival and reign in his stead.

It was thus to the rivalry among members of the

princely caste that the ancient Russian republics chiefly owed the preservation of their liberty; and the more important cities, which by their example naturally influenced the others, could always, by very reason of their extent, and the eagerness with which their suffrages were sought, turn this rivalry to the best account.

The relations that prevailed between the prince and the *vetche* explain how, in older Russia, freedom so complete and democratic was maintained without effort and without internal strife. All other republics, either of antiquity or of the Middle Ages, were, so to speak, limited republics or constitutional democracies, the will of the people being always more or less controlled by other social forces, while our early Russian republics were absolute and unlimited democracies. The people were supreme; every citizen had an equal voice in the government of the country, and neither the ruling prince, nor any other public functionary, had a vested interest in his place. The *vetche* could annul all or any of his decrees. Though he appointed officers to assist him in the administration, the *vetche* controlled his choice and could dismiss his nominee. They were not protected by the prince, and the *vetche* no more hesitated to punish a prince's nominee than a functionary elected by themselves. Neither the prince nor any other servant of the State was appointed for a fixed term. All held their places at the pleasure of the people. The bishops alone were nominally elected for life, but even they were sometimes summarily dismissed by the *vetche*. Thus the *vetche* was the sovereign power which regulated all the affairs of the country. There was no divided authority; the *vetche* spoke the voice and expressed the will of the people. In a word, the republics of ancient Russia were primitive states, elementary in their institutions, and purely democratic in their government.

CHAPTER III.

IF from the fragmentary notices dispersed through-out our old chronicles we endeavour to draw a living picture of these same *vetches,* the primitive and simple character of our ancient republican *régime* will be rendered more visible and striking.

On the banks of the river Volchow, and not far from Lake Ilmen, lies the famous city of Novgorod —now only a small provincial "chief-town" with some 18,000 inhabitants, but centuries ago one of the greatest of European cities, worthy, by its power and riches, of being called the Northern Venice. In the fourteenth and fifteenth centuries Novgorod was the capital of a vast republic, which included the northern half of modern Russia, stretching as far as the Ural mountains, and containing large towns and important cities. Favoured by its splendid position on the great highway which united Mediæval Europe with

the Levant, Novgorod the Great waxed rich and
powerful on the commerce and industry of her sons,
and for centuries successfully defended her liberties
against the ever-growing power of the Muscovite
Tzars. It was not until the sixteenth century that
the resistance of the heroic republic was finally
overcome. None of our old republics ever attained
to the same power and splendour as Novgorod the
Great, and none has left us records so rich of a
glorious past. In these priceless documents we find
the best material for the study of our early institutions.

On one of the squares of the now depopulated city,
the stranger is shown the place where, at the stroke
of the great bell which was there suspended, the
sovereign people were wont to meet. Its sacred
rope was free to all, every citizen being competent
to summon the *vetche* for deliberation on any subject affecting the welfare of individuals or the State.
The people were masters, even, as we have seen,
despots, sometimes violent and hasty, but always
noble and generous, like legendary Oriental kings,
fathers of their country, ever accessible to the
humblest of their subjects, ever ready to redress
their wrongs, and prompt to punish the trespasses of
the great and powerful. If none dared disturb for
trivial or inadequate cause the repose of the sleep-

ing lion, none, on the other hand, could hinder the humblest burgher from convoking the people and making complaint of any injustice committed against him ; and forcing the aggressor—whosoever he might be, whether *posadnik* (lord mayor) or prince—to appear and answer to the charge.

The rules touching the convocation of the *vetche* were few and simple, its meetings being marked by an almost entire absence of formality. Supreme power was vested in the entire body of the people, and wherever and whenever they met their will was law. There are instances on record of the militia of Novgorod while encamped in the face of the enemy constituting themselves into a *vetche,* and adopting resolutions which were held as binding as if they they had been passed by the assembled citizens in the great square of the capital.

But that which differentiates our ancient *vetche,* as well as our *mirs,* from all similar assemblies is the absence of, any system of voting. In every other republic, however free or democratic it might be—at Sparta and Rome, as well as at Athens and Florence —voting in one shape or another existed, and the principle that the minority should conform to the rule of the majority was the basis of all their political procedure. In the Slav nature there seems something antagonistic to this principle. I say Slav,

and not Russian, because among all the peoples of
that race, possessed of genuinely free institutions,
we invariably find that the principle of unanimous
decision is the only principle which the popular conscience is able to accept. In Poland these principles
were embodied in an unalterable law, than which
nothing could be more fatal and absurd. In the
national Polish diets, if one man—who might be
bribed by a foreign enemy—shouted his *liberum veto*,
it sufficed to annul the decision of the entire assembly. In the Ruthenian republics—those of the
Ukranian Cossacks on either side of the Dnieper,
and in warlike Zaporogia—the principle of unanimity
equally prevailed, and the system of legislation by
vote was never practised. There were, however,
occasions in which the more numerous, or, at any
rate, the stronger party found an effective way of
overcoming opposition. When some burning question
arose—for instance, the choice of a military chief
or higher magistrate—and none of the disputants
would yield, they generally came to blows, and so
soon as the physically weaker party had been sufficiently belaboured, they abandoned their opposition,
the desired unanimity was attained, and the candidates were elected by acclamation. These disputes
were sometimes settled in a manner still more
summary—with knife instead of fist. The *vetche* of

old Russia, especially those of Novgorod the Great, as to which we have more complete information than any other, seem to have been also at times very turbulent. The chroniclers tell of frequent disputes, some of which ended in sanguinary struggles and loss of life. But these cases were evidently exceptional. The republic could not have existed, much less prospered and grown in power, if civil war had been chronic in its capital. As a rule, moderate counsels prevailed, and differences were pacifically settled by persuasion and mutual concession. The mildness and docility of the Slav character rendered possible the application, on a large scale, of a principle based on an undeniably generous sentiment—respect for the rights of minorities, a sentiment declared by an eminent English political writer to be the foundation of true liberty.

CHAPTER IV.

SURVIVAL OF SELF-GOVERNMENT.

WE find, then, in the governing bodies of our ancient states the same striking peculiarity which distinguishes the humble assemblies of our obscure villages —the legislation by unanimous decision.

Nor, as reference to our first chapter will show, is this the only feature common to the *vetche* and the *mir*. The resemblance extends to details; their identity is almost complete, a surprising and remarkable fact when it is considered how different are the circumstances of these two institutions, and by how long an interval of time they are separated— the one perished centuries ago, the other still survives. In its methods of procedure, as well as by the primitive variety of its functions and the disorderly character of its proceedings, the obsolete *vetche* is neither more nor less than the modern commune assembly, and, though on a much larger scale, without any essential difference in its organization. If there be one nor payment of the other. For these reasons Russian governments have been compelled to recognize the rural communes, to confirm their privileges, treat with them as independent corporations, and allow them to manage their own affairs. The land register was kept by the communes, and not by individual proprietors; the taxes were based on the register, and paid by the village in its corporate capacity. If a villager went away and ceased therefore to contribute his quota to the common fund, the Government made no difference, always exacting the same amount until a new register was prepared, which might not be for years.

Such is the fiscal system which has been followed by the successive rulers of Russia—princes, khans, tzars, and emperors. No other system was possible. Even serfage did not interfere with rural self-government, and the great seigneurs, who owned both the land and bodies of the tillers of the soil, never attempted to restrict the autonomy of the commune. None of the political troubles which have swept over the country have affected the *mir* any more than the fierce winds which sweep over the ocean disturb the eternal calm of its lowmost depths. The *mir* can be touched only by the new methods of the present economic *régime*, a subject on which I cannot dwell in the present work.

The survival of self-government among the lower orders is a highly significant fact, proving as it does the political as well as the economic vitality of our communes, and accounting for the re-appearance of our old republican institutions every time the Russian people are free to manage their own affairs. Of this there are many instances.

In the thirteenth and fourteenth centuries, the time of the Muscovite autocracy's greatest development, tens of thousands of outlaws, fleeing from unbearable oppression, found a refuge on the steppes of Yaik (now Oural), the Don and the Dnieper. These fugitives, who called themselves Cossacks, founded a number of little military republics, identical in almost every respect with the purely Russian republics of which Novgorod was the most illustrious example. The chief difference consisted in the fact that the Cossack communities, having no princely families to supply them with rulers, elected military chiefs, who, under the titles of *ataman, hetman, koshevoi,* performed functions similar to those performed by the Rurikovetchi princes of ancient Russia. Even in our own time, whenever, as occasionally happens (for instance in 1830 at Staraia Roussa and other districts, and in 1856 in the province of Orel), a rising is temporarily successful, the insurgents never place themselves under the authority of a chief, but set up immediately a republic, *sui generis*, and supreme power is vested in a popular assembly.

Returning to our first theme, and with all the facts before us, we may affirm with full confidence that those who, judging solely by appearances, say that the Russian people have an instinctive preference for despotic government, make a great mistake. On the contrary, all their habits and tendencies, as revealed in their history, show them to possess a decided bent for freedom and strong aptitudes for self-government, wherein the vast majority of the nation are trained from childhood, and which, whenever they have the opportunity, Russian people spontaneously practise.

But what is, then, their monarchism, their devotion to the Tzar of which so much is said? The monarchism of Russian peasants is a conception which has exclusive reference to the State in its entirety, the whole body politic. If the peasants were left to themselves and free to realize their strange ideals, they would tell the White Tzar to remain on the throne, but they would send to the right about, and probably massacre, every governor, policeman, and *tchinovnik* in the land, and set up a series of democratic republics. For the peasants in their ignorance do not understand how Russia at large can govern herself; they do not see that the bureaucracy which they hate and the Tzar whom they love are essential parts of the same system, and that to destroy the former and leave the latter would be like cutting off the hands and feet and leaving the head and trunk. This is a misconception arising from simple ignorance, a misconception which, as instruction spreads among the people, will give place to truer ideas.

Yet it was not always so. A misconception can neither endure through five centuries nor be created by imagination. In the history and social conditions of the country must be sought the causes to which the autocracy owes its being, which maintain it, and form the historic justification of its existence; for there was a time when autocracy was the popular ideal and the centre of all the aspiration of the nation.

CHAPTER V.

THE MAKING OF THE DESPOTISM.

By what process was the ultra-democratic *régime* that prevailed in Russia during the eleventh and twelfth centuries transmuted in the course of three or four hundred years into a despotism of which it may well be affirmed, without historic exaggeration, the world has never seen the like?

To answer this question in detail it would be necessary to give a complete history of the development of the Muscovite monarchy. But so great an undertaking is beyond the scope of my present work; I must content myself with such brief sketch as will suffice to show that this unfortunate result is no fortuitous or accidental event, and that my description of our ancient liberties is in no respect overdrawn.

The organization of the central power in the oldest and most developed of our states—Novgorod the

Great—was, as we have seen, of an extreme primitiveness and simplicity. Not alone may the entire controlling authority—that is to say the *vetche*—but the entire state may be likened to one of those plants which, notwithstanding their size, are composed of a single cell. The dominions of the Novgorod greatly surpassed those of the Queen of the Adriatic. They were always growing by the accretion of colonies, either conquered by arms or acquired by treaty from the wild aboriginals. Some of these colonies, waxing in wealth and population, became in their turn powerful communities. Hence the establishment of a perfect understanding—a *modus vivendi*—between them and the mother city, was one of the most pressing social needs of the time, and essential to the integrity of the State. But what did ancient Russia to meet this necessity? Nothing at all. The colonies were regarded as integral parts of the metropolis, and the colonists were free to come to the capital whenever it pleased them and join in the deliberations of the *vetche*. When matters of importance were about to be discussed they were informed betimes and invited to attend. But if the colonists came not the Assembly decided all the same, giving no more heed to their special interests than to those of any other citizens who were hindered by unavoidable causes from being present. A colony, in fact,

was looked upon as being in some sort a quarter of
the city. It was even denominated *pregorod*, a word
which, literally rendered, signifies a ward of the
capital, albeit these curious wards might be distant
therefrom a month's journey. True, each colony had
a *vetche* of its own which regulated all local affairs ;
on the other hand, general legislation was the prerogative of the metropolitan Assembly, which, as the
supreme authority, the colonists were compelled in
the last resort to obey. The issues of peace or war
were also in the hands of the greater *vetche*. "That
which the elder ordered the younger had to do,"
says the old chronicler. So long as they were young
and struggling the colonists submitted. But so soon
as they felt themselves strong enough to walk alone
they dismissed the governor appointed by the metropolitan *vetche*, chose in his stead a prince with a
good *drugina*, and declared themselves independent.
Sometimes the separation was effected peacefully.
Generally, however, the old *vetche* and the new State
came to blows, and if the rebellious colony succeeded
in maintaining its pretensions by force of arms, its
independence was definitively acknowledged. It rose
at once from the position of a ward to that of a
"younger brother," and the two communities entered
into an alliance, and swore eternal friendship—proceedings which of course did not in the least hinder

them from falling out on the first occasion. No
lessons of wisdom were drawn from these frequent
scissions, and when in course of time the severed
colonies founded other colonies, the process of disin-
tegration went on as before. Thus in older Russia
the interior development of the country resulted, as
by the operation of a natural law, in the creation of
an ever growing number of small independent states,
which though republics in fact were principalities in
form. The multiplication of royal families also contributed in no small degree to this outcome; for
ambitious young princes, eager for power and place,
were always at hand ready to encourage separation
and stir up revolt.

Something like this, although due to an altogether
different cause, came to pass in some other countries.
The issue, however, in both cases was the same—the
creation of autocracy. Like the feudal barons, these
independent princes warred incessantly among themselves. Sometimes they were helped by the citizens.
But when the citizens were indifferent or hostile they
trusted to their own *drugina* and contingents of
mercenary nomads, whom they enlisted in their service. At last the country, devastated by these eternal
feuds, demanded peace at any price. The simplest
and easiest, and in existing circumstances the only
way of reaching this end, was the substitution of a

single prince for the multitude of princelings. For it is only by long training, intellectual growth, and material development that communities become habituated to the complex and costly mechanism of representative institutions, the only means hitherto discovered whereby union and independence can be reconciled with national security and personal freedom. Old Russia, which had not even learned the alphabet of this difficult lesson, was constrained like other peoples to undergo the hard apprenticeship of despotic government. The social and political condition of the country, moreover, rendered the establishment of autocratic rule both easier and more urgent than elsewhere—more urgent because the Russia of that day had not alone to contend with internal disorders, but to make head against incessant invasion. These invasions, dangerous and vexatious at the beginning of Russian history in the tenth and eleventh centuries, became in the twelfth century, when feeble nomads were succeeded by fierce Tartars, terrible and almost fatal; and only after a struggle of five hundred years was the country finally freed from their yoke and relieved from their aggressions.

On the other hand, the social condition of Russia offered fewer obstacles to union under a single sovereign than most other countries. The ordinary process of consolidation was through conquest and

the gradual annexation of neighbouring states, a
process which, depending as it did on the uncertain
fortunes of war, was necessarily slow and difficult.
Small independent states generally defended themselves vigorously and long. The powerful local aristocracy, dreading to sink into the position of a provincial
nobility, threw in their lot with the princes; and the
people, oblivious to their own interests, often joined
hands with the great against those who were wrongly
stigmatized as foreign enemies. The segregation of
their lives gave rise to petty local differences, which,
together with the ignorance natural to the age, produced in turn a crop of hatred and jealousy. It was
only with the help of the industrial classes that the
monarchies of Central Europe were enabled to overcome these hostile influences and complete the process
of unification by the consolidation of their kingdoms.

In Russia the process of unification took a different
course. If there were no burghers—no trading classes
—there were, on the other hand, fewer obstacles.
The agricultural population was only in part sedentary.
The quantity of unoccupied land was so vast, the art
of husbandry so backward, that the people were half
nomad. After burning the forests, they raised in the
rudest fashion such crops as they needed. When
the soil was exhausted, or they wanted a change,
they moved elsewhere; and this process they were

continually repeating. A peasant was always willing to exchange fields with a neighbour, or even
migrate to another province. The agricultural classes
roamed at will over the vast Russian plains in search
of a more fruitful soil or less onerous conditions.
Entire villages disappeared from one place to re-
appear in another. The political condition of the
time, as was natural, determined the general direction
of this great human flood. After the irruption of the
Tartars it flowed chiefly towards the north-west, where
the principalities of Vladimir, Tver, and Moscow had
constituted themselves into a state, and formed a
settled government. But in addition to the main
stream there were always minor currents flowing
between provinces of the same region. This coming
and going, this ebb and flow of peoples, by welding
the population into a homogeneous whole, greatly
facilitated the unification of the country. The peasants of Tver, Kazan, and Viatka came in time to
differ in nothing from the peasants of Nijni Novgorod.
Such a country as this afforded little room for the
development of those peculiar prejudices and strong
local ties by which populations that remain long
in the same place and become rooted in the soil
are invariably characterized. As for the higher or
warrior class, which was at once the head and nerve
force of the country, they were even more vagabond

and had fewer local ties than the peasants; for the ancient *drugina*, though they received grants of land " for food," were attached to the person of the prince, and not to the soil. Yet they were always volunteers, free fighters, who had the same right to change their prince as a workman to change his master; a right which they largely used, never scrupling to abandon a chief whose star had begun to wane for one whom fortune was beginning to favour. In these circumstances an annexation was generally little more than taking possession of a territory which, by reason of the defection of its military defenders, and the migration of great part of the population to the principality of a more powerful ruler, could offer no resistance to an invader. It often befell, moreover, that a prince whose independence was endangered would anticipate his fate, and avoid the consequences of defeat in the field by proceeding to Moscow, and voluntarily surrendering his dominions to his former rival, securing, as the reward of his homage and submission, riches, honour, and the title of boyar. At the court of Moscow the families of boyar princes, all descended from once independent sovereigns, may still be counted by the dozen.

Thus, as I have observed, the method by which unification was accomplished in Russia differed from that by which it was accomplished in most other countries. It may be considered as partaking in equal measure of the gathering of nomad tribes around the standard of a valiant and successful chieftain, and the process peculiar to countries whose populations are completely sedentary. This explains at once the extreme facility with which Muscovite unification was accomplished and the origin of the despotism that followed in its wake.

While the political condition of Russia and the exigencies of a life and death struggle extending over four centuries, a struggle with enemies of an alien race and a hostile religion, converted the chief of the state into a permanent military dictator—so loyally supported by his people that to oppose him was regarded as a crime—the social condition of the country lent to the despotism so terrible a conservative force that, long after its energies had begun to decline, and the causes that brought it into being, which causes, to a certain point, justified its existence, ceased to prevail, the Tzars were enabled to retain all their autocratic powers and continue their encroachments on the rights of their subjects.

The ideal Muscovite state was an army, a colossal *drugina* transformed into a military caste, and disseminated in quarters over all the vast area of the empire. Divided by immense distances, this class was divided still further by the rivalry which prevailed between one clan or section and another, and among the members of the clans themselves. It had nothing in common with feudal aristocracies, their hierarchies of nobles, and their dependent vassals. Neither did it resemble the class of Polish magnates, who maintained at their own charge thousands of poor knights trained to arms, and attached to their patron by a community of origin and interest. The country was too poor to enable the boyars to indulge in costly luxuries, and too extensive to permit the smaller nobility to flock to the palaces of wealthy potentates. The Tzar, moreover, could always recompense their services by grants of land, and confirm their allegiance by hopes of advancement. All the immense material forces of the State were thus represented by a vast horde, dependent, both individually and in mass, directly on the Tzar, and living only by his favour—a horde of whom the inferior ranks were always ready to crush at a sign any show of resistance on the part of their superiors to their master's behests.

And all this in a country where two centuries and a half of slavery had destroyed among the upper classes every sentiment of honour and dignity, and among the lower even the memory of their ancient liberties, habituating them to bow in humble submission to brute force, whereas the turbulent and irascible Russian of the olden time was always prompt to resent injustice with rebellion.

True, the same natural conditions which hindered the formation of permanent social ties prevented the central government from making its authority effectively felt over the whole extent of its wide-stretching dominions. The greater part of the nation, even the greater part of the military caste, felt only fortuitously the power of the Tzar. All the more terrible was the position of those whom he had within his grasp, for the autocracy had developed into a despotism which was distinguished less by the greatness of its power than by the boundlessness of its absolutism. What resistance could oppose to it the miserable upper class, formed as it was of boyars, men without either strength in themselves or support in the country, menials of mongrel stock, who had flocked from the four winds of heaven in search of honours and money, with nothing in common save a desire to win the favour of the Tzar, and the fear of being distanced by more crafty or fortunate rivals? Servility and sycophancy, a ready proneness to every sort of baseness and humiliation, were the sole passports to prosperity, and often the only means of saving their heads. Unlike the similar classes of other countries, the Russian nobility, instead of moderating and opposing the despotism of the Crown, were either its victims, its instruments, or its advocates. Moscow became, in some sort, a vast alembic, where, under pressure of the iron circle that enclosed them, despotism and servility were elaborated, *motu proprio*, by the reciprocal action of the ingredients of which they were composed. Having made a step in advance, and seeing all prostrate themselves at its feet, absolutism took the second step. The habits acquired by the fathers became instincts with the sons, who transmitted them augmented and intensified to their successors. The only limits to this development were the tastes and inclinations of the despots themselves. But the latter being as barbarous as the times in which they lived, and having before them the example of their still more savage Tartar predecessors, wrought havoc with every human right, as regardless of personal dignity and honour as of every other virtue which distinguishes men from brutes, until the monstrous result was reached which made the rule of Tzars a disgrace to our common nature.

CHAPTER VI.

THE POWER OF THE CHURCH.

WE shall, however, be far from understanding the strength, the character, and the durability of the Muscovite despotism if, in addition to its exterior and material influences, we do not take into account that deeper moral influence which gives governments so firm a hold over the human heart—the sanction of religion.

From the very beginning of our political life the Russian clergy have possessed great influence, for it was they, and the Christianity which they taught, that were the means of introducing the rudiments of culture among the then savage inhabitants of the land. Priests and monks were the masters and counsellors both of princes and subjects. Nevertheless, in the eleventh and twelfth centuries Greco-Slav culture began to take root in the country, and, side by side with the clerical schools, laymen, who gave themselves diligently to study, founded secular

schools, even for girls, in every principal town. But
successive Tartar invasions utterly destroyed these
first germs of secular learning, and, according to the
testimony of our historians, the Russia of the sixteenth
century was far less cultured and more barbarous than
the Russia of the twelfth. Even among the higher
aristocracy the arts of reading and writing became
rare accomplishments, and at the diet held in the
reign of John IV. there were princes of the blood who
were unable to sign their names.

It was the policy of the Tartars, as of most
conquering races, to respect the religion of the
conquered. One of the first decrees of the Khans
accorded full and entire immunity to churches,
monasteries, and priests. Study was confined exclusively to the sacristy and the convent, and so late
as the seventeenth century the clergy alone were
acquainted with letters.

If there had been nothing else, the possession of this
advantage would have sufficed to confer upon church-
men an influence altogether exceptional, and their
power was still further increased by their social and
political position. It was to the clergy that the people,
when they had incurred the displeasure of the Almighty,
betook themselves for consolation. It was the clergy
who encouraged them in the hour of defeat, and animated them with promises of victory in the sacred

warfare against their infidel conquerors. Their two strongest passions were religious fanaticism and patriotic ardour, and of these passions the Church was at once the personification and the expression. It was the monks, again, who roused the too timorous princes to rebellion against the Tartar oppressors, and stories of saintly and fearless anchorites who themselves took up the sword to combat the enemies of Christ still live in legend and song. In a word, it was the clergy who put themselves at the head of every national movement; and when victory smiled on the Muscovite arms, it was the Church that reaped the richest reward.

And now the all-powerful clergy, who hold in their hands the ingenuous and confiding soul of the nation, have become faithful servitors of the despot and ardent supporters of absolutism.

The Russian religion was from the beginning an essentially national religion, differing in this respect from that of all other European countries, where the Church was an international institution, directed by a single chief who called himself the "King of kings," and whose members, whatever their race, held the same belief, and looked to each other for sympathy and support. For these reasons Russia has suffered less than most other countries from spiritual usurpations and ecclesiastical abuses. On the other hand, her Church has been completely subjugated by the despotic power, and made an ignoble instrument of tyranny and oppression. Theologians are pleased to say that the Tzar is not the head of the Russian Church, that she recognizes no other head than Jesus Christ. Be it so. Yet to draw from this abstract theory practical conclusions is counting without the host. As a matter of fact, in a despotic country where the *persons and bodies* of the clergy are at the mercy of a sovereign who has power of appointment and deposition, and may exile them, put them to the torture or to death at the least caprice—as the Muscovite Tzars have often done—in such a country as this the pretended independence of the Church is a delusion and a fraud. This John IV. abundantly proved. For that amiable monarch, not content with strangling the metropolitan of the Russian Church, and flogging hundreds of priests to death at Novgorod, compelled ecumenical councils to sanction practices and doctrines which the canons and the apostles condemned as abominations.

But the Tzars had rarely need to constrain the clergy to obedience by force. They had only to choose the most zealous of the mitred crowd who were always offering their services. For the education of our clergy, being based exclusively on the literature and history of the Byzantine despotism, they had and could have no other political ideal than an unlimited monarchy. And when John III. took to wife Sophia Paleologus, the last scion of the imperial Greek dynasty, the Russian clergy imputed to their Tzar the heirship of the Sancro-sanct eastern emperors and of all their glory and authority. The exaltation and *culte* of absolutism became thenceforth their historic mission—a mission which, in season and out of season, and among every class of the people, they have faithfully and zealously performed.

Religious propaganda is the sure, the last, and most potent of the influences which confer on the Muscovite autocracy its sacred character and its tremendous power. The circumstance arising from the hard necessities of an unfortunate political life, strengthened by social conditions which enlisted on the side of despotism every selfish instinct—ambition, cupidity, and fear—were approved, ennobled, and exalted by the supreme sanction of the Church. Obedience to the Tzar was proclaimed as the first duty and highest virtue of the Christian believer. The Tzar, on his part, almost believed himself to be an incarnation of the Divinity. Herberstein, the well-known traveller, when he visited Moscow, was greatly struck by the sacred character so implicitly imputed to the sovereign power. "If you ask a Muscovite," he said, "any question which he is unable to answer, he is almost

sure to say, 'God and the Tzar only know!' And
the Tzar himself, if he were asked anything—for
instance, the pardon of a prisoner—would be almost
sure to say : 'We shall release him if it be the will of
God.'" As if he had a perfect understanding with
the Deity, and their relations were of the most familiar
and confidential character! God's will meant, of
course, his will. According to the Russian priests,
their Divine Master acted in some sort as their earthly
master's obedient genii, prompt to punish every
infraction, open or secret, of the orders of his terrestrial
vicegerent, and ready to recompense with eternal
bliss all who suffered patiently and humbly the un-
deserved and unjust punishments which the Tzar, by
reason of human fallibility or the fault of his agents,
might sometimes inflict. There is no irony in this.
It is sober truth. In an extant letter written by
John IV., the philosopher of this doctrine, to Prince
Kourbski, he charges it against him as a sin that he
escaped from the clutches of his sacred majesty, in
these words : "If you are a just and God-fearing
man, as you say, tell me why you have fled, instead
of receiving from my hand the torture and the
death which would procure you a place in heaven ?"
And the worst of it was that these monstrous ideas
were not held by the tyrant alone ; they were shared
by his people. Though that ferocious brute John

IV. made his reign a very orgie of cruelty, murder, and lust; though as cowardly as he was vile—seeing everywhere about him conspiracies against his life— he scourged to death thousands of his subjects, and inflicted on them tortures of which even to read makes the blood run cold; though the libidinous tyrant violated the wives and daughters of his boyars, killing all who showed the least unwillingness, and though his infamies went on for forty years without surcease, not once during his monstrous reign was protest made, not a single hand raised either to hinder or avenge these shameful outrages. Historians have not been able to discover the slightest trace of any plot against John IV. His victims might sometimes flee, but resist or conspire—never.

And yet these men were not cowards. For the most part brave warriors, celebrated for their exploits in the field, they often showed in the torture-chamber and on the scaffold high qualities of endurance and courage, and rare strength of mind. But by a perversion of their intellectual faculties, due to their training, this strength of mind served no other purpose than to overcome the natural impulse to rebellion and restrain their indignation against the Tzar, to whom abject submission was the sacred ideal which had been held before them from their earliest youth. When Prince Kepnin, after being impaled, was

dying a slow death in atrocious suffering, he sang—
the miserable wretch—sang hymns in honour of the
Tzar, his master and murderer !

These are the services which have been rendered
to the Russian nation by their Church. During all
the ages of the existence of the Russian State she has
been faithful to her self-imposed and degrading trust.
What more natural than that at the first awakening
of political conscience in the instructed classes, their
first words were words of malediction against religion !
What more just than now, when the first gleam of
the light of culture is reaching the people, they should
abandon in thousands the faith of their forefathers !

CHAPTER VII.

Muscovy became a veritable theocracy. True the Tzar did not celebrate the mass, yet he united in his person all the attributes of an absolute king and of a chief of the State as irresponsible as a Tartar Khan, and as infallible as a Roman Pontiff. Nothing but the power of a dominant priesthood could have effected this wonderful transformation of the *ci-devant con-dottieri* chiefs, such as were once the ancestors of the imperial family, into earthly monarchs with heavenly attributes.

The reign of the latter Tzars of the Rurik dynasty was the hot youth period of the autocracy, which had only just emerged from the foam and agitation that accompanied the formation of the State. In the subsequent period, that of the Romanoff Tzars, the despotism, now fully matured, reached the last phase of its development. Sure of itself and confident in

the future, it now threw off the roughness and violence
that characterized the first epoch of its existence.
It ceased to fear and suspect, and became as immov-
able, absolute, and inevitable as a law of nature.

But theocracy means stagnation. The Russian
people, it should be remembered, adopted the Christianity of the Greek rite, while all other European
peoples gathered round the banner of Rome. Now in
the popular idea, and, above all, in that of the clergy
—who are nowhere distinguished for tolerance—this
was equivalent to saying that the Russians were the
only nation who held the true faith of Christ. They
were thus immeasurably superior to all neighbouring
peoples — schismatics, heretics, and unbelievers,
without exception. And when in course of time
Russia acquired force and splendour, not alone freeing
herself from the infidel yoke, but attacking her former
oppressors, and conquering one after another the
Tartar tribes, religious exaltation was reinforced with
patriotic pride. The Russian people were evidently
God's elect, who, after having proved them in the fiery
furnace of slavery, was now raising them up above all
other nations. To keep His favour and deserve His
blessing, what else could they do but follow the
example of their forefathers, and guard intact the
holy faith which had brought them so many benefits,
and marked them out as His chosen people ?

The clergy, whose bigotry was only exceeded by their ignorance, did not content themselves with conducting public worship and attending to the strict duties of their priestly calling. Like the odour of rancid oil, they penetrated everywhere, soiling all they touched, and petrifying everything they pretended to bless. It was declared a mortal sin to change or modify any custom or practice inherited from the past. Nothing was too minute to escape their attention, and there was no single usage which they did not attempt to control. Dress, the fashion of wearing the hair, the preparation of food—trifles light as air—were gravely discussed by reverend ecclesiastics and canonized by ecumenical councils, composed of the flower of the clergy under the presidency of the metropolitan, councils which have left behind them, in a document of a hundred chapters, an ineffaceable record of human folly and their own stupidity.

Priests and people, being thus clothed in perfection from head to foot, had naturally nothing to learn from miscreant *nemzi* (mutes), as all foreigners were indiscriminately called (a word now exclusively reserved for Germans). They could only contaminate the national purity.

Thus did clerical fanaticism raise up a barrier between Russia and the rest of Christian Europe

more difficult to surmount than the great wall of
China. Catholics and Protestants were regarded as
being little better than heathens and Mohammedans.
Contact with them was sinful. When these mis-
believers visited the country on business, they had to
live in separate quarters, like Jews in the Middle
Ages. Their relations with the natives were limited
to occasions of strict necessity, and they might not
prolong their stay in the country beyond a limited
time fixed beforehand. The envoys of foreign
governments, who came from time to time on affairs
of state, were placed under continual supervision.
The access to them of unauthorized persons was
barred by cordons of police, who beset their houses
night and day. When they walked through the
streets, people shunned them as if they had the
plague, and fled in all directions—of course in
obedience to orders—and ministers and others who
visited the " foreign devils " in an official capacity,
ran a very real risk of being charged with the dire
crimes of heresy and witchcraft.

Muscovy, in truth, was sinking into a veritable
Chinese torpor. The more the country indulged in
self-admiration, the more it tried to preserve itself
from contact with the West, the deeper it relapsed
into barbarism. All the travellers who visited Russia
in the seventeenth century were struck by the low-

ness of its culture and the backwardness of its civilization. At a time when Western Europe was covered with universities, and printing-presses were found in every city, copying with the pen was the only method of multiplying books practised by the Muscovites. In 1563 the first printing-office introduced into the country was closed by order of the clergy, who regarded it as an invention of the devil; and the compositors, John Fedoroff and Peter Mstislavez, only escaped prosecution for necromancy by flight. Arabic numerals, introduced into Europe in the twelfth century, were not used in Russia until the seventeenth.

Every industry was equally backward; and two centuries after gunpowder had come into general use, many of the soldiers of the Tzar still fought with bows and arrows—even when the national territory had become so extensive that the army required for its defence, and the consequent outlay on its maintenance, had increased threefold within a hundred years. Wars, moreover, being conducted at greater distances from the capital, were waged with greater difficulty and at much greater cost. Up to the beginning of the seventeenth century, Russia enlarged her borders towards the East. She now began to advance in the opposite direction, and came in contact with the civilized and powerful

peoples of the West, against whom her army and
her military equipment, however efficient against
nomad Asiatic tribes, were of no avail.

Hence arose demands which the natural resources
of the country were inadequate to meet, and burdens
were laid on the people heavier than they could bear.
The reign of Tzar Alexis (father of Peter the Great),
when the Muscovite Empire received its greatest
accessions of territory, witnessed also, and from this
very cause, a social and economic crisis of unexampled
severity.

Never before had the people been so heavily taxed.
Multitudes of townsfolk and peasants, unable to meet
the calls of the State, abandoned their fields and their
homes and fled whither they could. This rendered
the lot of those who were left behind still harder
to bear. They had to pay both their own taxes
and those of their fugitive neighbours. Many of
the unfortunates died under the tax-gatherer's stick,
and hundreds of villages were deserted and their
inhabitants dispersed all over the country. It
was sought to combat the evil by issuing savage
edicts against vagabondage ; but the only effect of
these measures seemed to be an increase in the number of vagabonds, and their conversion into brigands.
The fugitives hid themselves in forests and desert
places, and, passing the frontier in crowds, took

refuge with the warlike Cossacks of the Dnieper and the Don. These turbulent settlers, who occupied the steppes once possessed by the Tartars, strengthened by so many new arrivals, renounced the passive part of refugees from oppression, and took up arms to avenge themselves on the country which had driven them forth. Then befell the terrible insurrection, led by the ferocious Cossack chief and popular hero, Stenka Rasin, who raised the whole of the south-west against the government of the Tzar, took several cities, put to the sword all the nobles and the wealthy who fell into his hands, and shook the very foundation of the Muscovite State. But when the fortunes of Russia seemed to be at their lowest ebb, the Cossack hordes were utterly routed by soldiers armed with modern weapons and instructed by German officers.

There were also popular movements arising from the same cause—the intolerable burden of taxation and the cruelty with which payment was enforced—in Novgorod, Pscov, and other parts of the country. Even in the capital the people rose several times in insurrection, and the Tzar could only pacify them by delivering for execution several of his favourite and most trusty councillors, to whom the populace, according to their wont, ascribed all their misfortunes.

It could no longer be doubted that a strain was being put on the country greater than it was able to

bear. To meet the new requirements of the State
and make head against the difficulties of the times, it
had become necessary to infuse new life into the
body politic and re-invigorate its exhausted members.
These ends could be attained only in one way—by
adopting the methods of European civilization, and,
with the help of industry and science, increasing the
productiveness of labour and developing the natural
forces of the nation. The need was so evident and
urgent that even the hard and superstitious ob-
scurantism of the Muscovite Government could no
longer bar the way of progress. In the reign of
Alexis, European civilization obtained a first footing
at Moscow. Encouragement was offered to foreigners ;
a whole colony of foreign artisans settled in the
capital, and a part of the army was drilled in German fashion and equipped with German weapons.
This was only the beginning; it was impossible to
put a limit to the advance of civilization. On the
other hand, progress in a country where a slight
change in the mode of dress was regarded as an enormous innovation could not be otherwise than tenta-
tive and slow, and history does not wait. Russia
was so much behind other nations, that if she had
wallowed in her superstitious stagnation a few generations longer she might never have recovered the lost
ground. Puissant German nations were growing up

at her borders; Prussia would have planted her foot firmly on the Baltic and barred for none can say how long Russia's one path to international commerce and European culture. The emergency could be met only by measures both efficacious and prompt, by the rough ways of revolution rather than by ordinary methods of reform. These measures were taken under the auspices of Tzar Peter, who has rightly been called "Great," and never was revolution more opportunely wrought.

CHAPTER VIII.

THE GREAT REFORMER.

THE career of Peter the Great is so well known in England that it is unnecessary here to recount his exploits. His work, it may be well to observe, was essentially political. Nothing could be more absurd than to represent the cruel reforming Tzar as a man of lofty sentiment, admiring civilization for itself, and desirous of introducing it into his empire for the intellectual improvement of his subjects. In order to render Russia equal to the fulfilment of her new destinies the first essential was to make her a strong state, and to this end Peter directed all his energies. Science, culture, and the arts he valued solely for their practical utility, caring for them only so far as they forwarded his political designs. The foremost of these designs was the organization of a powerful military force, well armed and disciplined, and supplied with equipments and material of war from

sources exclusively Russian. The sciences that Peter
protected and the schools which he founded were
such as promised to give him good officers, engineers,
and administrators. The industries he most favoured
were those which provided for the wants of his army
and navy, and contributed most largely to the revenues of the State. The new culture retained this
essentially material character for more than a
hundred years, a period during which it enjoyed
the unswerving patronage and support of the Government. It was not until near the middle of the
eighteenth century, when German ideas were in some
measure superseding French influence, that broader
views and a more liberal and humane conception of
culture began to obtain, a change which the Government regarded with the reverse of satisfaction.

But to introduce by force a new civilization—even
in an exclusively material form—it was needful to
enter into close relations with foreigners, break de-
cisively with the past, and scout all the traditions
and superstitions of the people, who in their re-
pugnance to reform were supported by the strongest
moral force the nation possessed—its religion. In
these circumstances half-measures would have been
useless. It was necessary to declare open war, not
alone against popular superstitions, but against the
priestly caste by whom they were encouraged and

maintained. This Peter did, and though on the part
of a theocratic Tzar a bold and audacious enterprize,
he succeeded to the full. The old ecclesiastical
organization was broken up, and the higher dignitaries of the Church who opposed reform were
replaced by less stiff-necked ecclesiastics borrowed
from the Orthodox Ukranian Church. But Peter's
victory, though complete, was not achieved without
loss. A Tzar who dragooned the Church, who fore-
gathered with heretics, dressed German fashion, and,
not content with cutting off his own beard, made his
courtiers cut off theirs, could not possibly command
the adoration which had been so willingly paid to his
predecessors. Peter was even declared to be anti-
christ, and it is highly significant of the social and
political condition of Russia that, while the unspeakable atrocities of John the Terrible did not
provoke even a show of resistance, Peter's reforms
provoked several outbreaks of open rebellion, favoured
by the clergy, and fomented by his more fanatical
opponents, some of whom even plotted against his
life. On the other hand, it is quite certain that
neither Peter nor any of his aftercomers could have
committed with impunity the abominations which
disgraced the reigns of some of the older Muscovite
Tzars. Paul I. was put to death by his own courtiers
for offences far less heinous than theirs had been ;

and there can be no question that the conversion of tzardom into an empire has restricted the arbitrary authority of the occupant of the throne. Though still powerful he is no longer a god.

Yet so far from the chief of the State having lost any of his sovereign prerogatives, the secularization of the government—if I may be allowed to use such a term—by putting a check on merely personal caprice, has increased tenfold the real power of the crown.

The Muscovite Tzars, like Oriental despots, might oppress and maltreat individuals to the full extent of their desires; but as touching institutions they were comparatively powerless, and had only a limited influence in public affairs. It is a striking fact that when men set up a master to whom they ascribe despotic authority and more than human attributes, they often succeed in neutralizing his power by very excess of devotion. They cripple him with impalpable chains. The courtiers of old Japan succeeded in persuading the Mikado that if he moved the world would fall in pieces. So the poor man, to prevent so terrible a calamity, remained on his throne for hours together without moving a limb, dropping an eyelid, or uttering a word; and though worshipped as a demigod, he was in reality more impotent and inoffensive than the meanest of his servants. If the ingenious Japanese could have prevailed on their Mikado to prolong his repose for fifteen hours, we should have had a perfectly original example of that contradiction in terms, a powerless despotism. They did not quite succeed, however, for the Mikado evaded the difficulty by leaving his crown when he quitted his place. Yet for devices of this sort the palm of originality must be conceded to the courtiers of Japan. Nowhere else has anything at once so simple and so effective been invented. But there is found in all despotisms something not unlike it—thanks to what people call etiquette, which is no more than an expedient for checking the activity of the monarch by making him waste so much time and energy in puerile and useless ceremonial observances that he is physically unable to give sustained attention to public affairs, which, whether he likes it or not, must be left in great measure to the uncontrolled management of ministers and courtiers. It was thus at the old French court, as M. Taine has so well described, and probably even more so at the court of Moscow. The only difference was that the Bourbon kings had to give most of their time to the mere ceremonial of etiquette—receptions, levées, dressing and eating in public, and so forth; while the Muscovite Tzars were greatly occupied with religious rites, masses, prayers, visits to the monasteries, and inspection of saintly relics. Then came

the regular routine of traditional observances, for in a
theocratic state everything is sacred—except the lives
and liberties of citizens. If the fancy took him, the
Tzar might lay a town in ashes, and put the population of an entire province to the sword; but he could
not, without exciting general disapprobation, neglect
the least of old customs or break the unwritten laws
of his court. He might behead a noble or bastinado
a boyar with impunity; but it was impossible for
him, without causing serious and lasting discontent,
to promote a man of plebeian birth to high office.
Tyrant as was John IV., he could confer only an
inferior title of nobility on Adashteff, the favourite of
his early years, simply because the latter happened
to be the son of an inferior officer; and it was not
until nearly the end of his reign that Alexis ventured
to raise his father-in-law and friend, Artamon Mat-
veeff—a simple country gentleman—to the dignity of
boyar. In order to reconcile the pretensions of birth
with the requirements of the public service a double
administration was created. Great boyars were made
ministers of state, but their functions were strictly
limited to military affairs, each of them being provided with a secretary of low rank and high capacity,
who did all the work and exercised all administrative
power. Those were the *diaki* and *sou-diaki* of evil
memory. Attached to every ministry were several of

these officers, who were formed into chambers or
colleges. The jealousies and conflicts that inevitably
arose between these heterogeneous elements greatly
impaired the efficiency of the service as an instrument
of government, the boyars being much given to exchange their part of drones for that of drags, to the
great detriment of the administrative machine and
the injury of the country.

The secularization of the State, though it lowered
the prestige of its chief as a theocratic sovereign,
freed him, on the other hand, from the galling fetters
of religious and governmental routine. The Tzar became master of his time, and could give the whole
of it to public affairs. Master also of his people, he
could make whatever appointments he thought fit.
His political power was thus largely increased, and
he was able to make the government really his own.
The Great Reformer wanted nothing more. Making
a clean sweep of antiquated and hierarchic pretensions, Peter never hesitated to pass over all his
nobles, and raise to the highest posts in his service
the obscurest plebeians, in whom he discerned high
capacity for affairs. His administration, organized
on the German model, with ramifications everywhere
depending only on the chief of the state, became
absolute and supreme. The entire nation—people,
nobles, and clergy—Peter seized in his strong grasp,

and did with them what he would. His one thought was to make Russia a powerful state. To this end he bent all his energies, and forced every interest and every class to co-operate in its accomplishment.

In old Moscow there was no standing army. The fortresses were occupied by arquebusiers, who, after finishing their term of service, returned to civil life. The army was composed chiefly of nobles, who received for their services grants of lands for life—sometimes, but very rarely, in fee simple. At the end of a war they always returned to their fields. But to place Russia on an equality with neighbouring countries, and enable Peter to carry out his plans, a permanent military force was indispensable. This object he effected in a manner equally simple and effective. By a single stroke of the pen he transformed his militia, composed of men who had enlisted under conditions altogether different, into a standing army, permanently embodied. To fill up the gaps in its ranks left by war, and provide fresh food for powder, he established the conscription, under the monstrous condition that the rank and file should serve with the colours for twenty-five years. The nobles were still more unfortunate. From the age of twenty those of them who were sound in mind and body were required, when called upon, to serve the State in one capacity or other, either as soldiers, sailors, or administrators, until death — only disablement by wounds or complete decrepitude giving them the right to return to their homes. And it was not alone bodily service that Peter required from his nobles ; they had to give also their intelligence, and to the end that they might give it effectively, they were ordered to be educated. All young men of noble birth were compelled to attend schools formed specially for their instruction. When they did not go voluntarily, soldiers were sent to fetch them. If they resisted they were flogged, and if their parents, too ignorant and superstitious to appreciate the advantages of culture, concealed them, they were flogged too. When the impressed scholars reached the age of twenty they were examined. Those who passed were eligible for superior appointments ; those who failed were condemned never to marry, and compelled to serve in the lower ranks of the navy.

To compensate the aristocratic class for this eternal bondage to the State, or rather to enable them to support the obligations laid on them by the Tzar, the estates, which had previously been tenable only for life, were made hereditary possessions in fee simple. But as the peasants always went with the land they cultivated, they became the serfs of their noble masters, to whom their relations had hitherto been those of vassal to seigneur than of serf to owner.

Before the rise of the Muscovite tzardom completely free, the Russian peasantry were gradually reduced to servitude by the great, and in the middle of the sixteenth century the Government took away from them the last vestige of their ancient liberties—the right of leaving one landowner at the end of the agricultural year and taking service with another. This privilege was greatly restrained by Tzar Boris, and finally abolished a century later by Tzar Alexis. The peasants were thenceforth absolutely forbidden to leave the masters to whom they were assigned by the State. They remained, however, on the land, for to have allowed them to be removed would have been an injury to the State. But after Peter's time the seigneurs could dispose of the peasants at their pleasure, and buy and sell them as they bought and sold their cattle ; and, provided the noble owner and his heirs male fulfilled their duties to the State, the latter never interfered. The peasants thus became, in the fullest sense of the word, the slaves of the nobles, and from that time dates the true slavery of the Russian nation.

For all were alike held in bondage to the State. From the nobles it required their blood, their time, and their lives. The people, besides giving many of their sons to the army, supported with enforced labour the Tzar's servants and their own masters, and sustained with the taxes wrung from their toil the

finances of government. Sometimes even they were
constrained to give the work of their hands ; as, for
instance, in the construction of the second capital,
which the Russian Reformer ordered to be built.
Multitudes of masons, excavators, carpenters, and
other labourers were summoned from every part of
the empire, and commanded, " under pain of confiscation of their goods and death on the scaffold,"
to raise on the banks of the Neva the great city
which bears the name of its founder. But how many
when traversing its spacious streets bestow a thought
on the hundred thousand nameless serfs at the cost
of whose lives St. Petersburg was built !

The reign of Peter was indeed a hard time for his
subjects. Never before were a people called upon by
sovereign to make such sacrifices of property and life
—sacrifices, it must be confessed, in great part wasted,
for though the Great Reformer's ideas were generally
luminous, his methods were often injudicious. He
seemed to prefer violence to moderation, even when
violence was not alone adverse to his interests but
fatal to his projects. But he did his work—Russia
became a powerful State. His irregular hordes, of
whom 85,000 had been utterly routed by 12,000
Swedes, were replaced by a standing, well-disciplined,
and well-equipped army of 180,000 men. He increased
the public revenues from three million roubles to

fourteen millions. So great, moreover, was the vigour imparted to the natives by European culture which he introduced, that its power and wealth have continued to grow from generation to generation. Notwithstanding the incapacity of most of Peter's many successors, Russia has maintained her position as a great power; and by her acquisitions on the Baltic and her conquest of the Euxine, she has assured to the Slav race permanent independence, and the development of a national culture most conformable to their social and intellectual genius.

This was the object, and this is the merit of the military dictatorship founded by Peter the Great. It was an historic necessity, the only remedy for the lethargy of the period produced by the theocratic stagnation of the old Muscovite *régime.*

CHAPTER IX.

BUT political forms, however suitable to one age and in one set of circumstances, become, in a later age and in other circumstances, not alone superfluous but hurtful. Instead of helping they hinder, instead of promoting progress they produce reaction. It was thus with the Russian autocracy.

In proportion as culture and civilization—following the impulse given by Peter—obtained foothold in the country and was accepted by the people, the element of coercion, which had been introduced into every department of public life, became less and less necessary, and finally lost altogether its right to be. In the time of the Great Reformer everything which had the least taint of "Germanism"—in other words, of European culture—had literally to be forced down people's throats. Boys were driven to school with whips, and invitations to court balls and *soirées* were accompanied by threats

of confiscation in the event of disobedience. For the
fathers and mothers of that age kept their daughters
under lock and key in Oriental fashion, and it was an
old custom, faithfully observed, to marry them to men
on whom they had never set eyes. Even personal
interest and desire for wealth were unable to cope
with the combined forces of indolence and superstition.

Russia was rich in mines, as well of gold as of the
less noble metals, hardly any of which had been
explored. When it became manifest that, in this
instance at least, self-interest was not a sufficient
incentive to exertion, the Emperor administered a
further stimulus—issued stringent decrees ordering
owners of mines, under divers penalties, to turn their
potential treasures to account, as well for their own
benefit as for that of the State. In the event of any
proprietors neglecting to obey this command private
individuals were authorized to open his mines and
appropriate his minerals, without either asking leave
or paying a royalty.

Another generation, and all was changed. Self-
interest, outgrowing superstition, no longer required
the spur of Government prescription! Landowners,
not content with working mines already discovered,
sought eagerly fresh sources of wealth. It was no
longer necessary to fine nobles who persisted in
wearing the national dress, nor to cut off their beards

by force, nor to drag people to balls and amusements
by the hair of their heads. The influence of fashion
and love of pleasure were proving more potent than
violence and threats. The masters of schools no
longer frightened parents and children out of their
senses, for the latter, now in their turn parents, were
eager to bestow on their children that education which
they had once regarded with aversion and alarm.
Thus in private life coercion came to an end, for the
very sufficient reason that there was nobody to coerce.

A similar result was wrought in the general functions of the State.

In the reign of Peter III. (1762), three generations
after the publication of the great Peter's ukase im-
posing involuntary service on the aristocratic class,
appeared another ukase known as the " Enfranchisement of the Nobles," whereby they were left free to
serve the State or not, as they pleased, without any
derogation of their rights and privileges. The reasons
assigned by the Government for this measure afford a
remarkable proof of the change which in less than a
century had come over the social condition of Russia.
In the emphatic language of the ukase it had been
needful, during the reigns of Peter and our immediate
successors, to constrain the nobles to render service
to the State, and compel them to instruct their
children; but the desire for education, being now

so general and so great, and the zeal of the upper classes for the public service having produced so many excellent and courageous captains and able administrators, the Emperor considered that the system of coercion had become superfluous, and ordered it to be abolished.

Though suggested mainly by a desire to please the nobility, this measure was fully justifiable on grounds of public policy. The number of men able and willing to serve the State being more than enough, it had become unnecessary, and therefore absurd, to use coercion, and neither then nor since have Russian Governments had to complain of a paucity of *tchinovniks* or military officers ; they have only had to "take their pick" from a host of competing candidates.

If the Government of that time had been moved solely by considerations of justice and of sound policy, the emancipation of the nobles would have been immediately followed by the emancipation of the peasants. For the latter were reduced from the condition of vassals to that of slaves solely to compensate the nobles for the obligatory service to the State imposed on them by Peter the Great. With their relief from this burden, the landowning class lost all right to the involuntary and unpaid labour of the tillers of the soil. It was perhaps an instinctive

conviction of this truth on the part of the peasants
that gave rise to the exaggerated hopes which cul-
minated in the widespread and frequent servile insur-
rections of the period. But abstract considerations
of equity have little weight in political evolutions.
Serfage, no longer needed in the interest of the
Government, was retained for the benefit of the
aristocracy.

At last came the turn of this institution. Serfage
was abolished in 1861. It would be impossible, even
it it were desired, to ignore the salient causes of this
great reform—on the one hand, the humane sentiments of our instructed society imbued with modern
ideas ; on the other, the wish to remove, once for all,
the danger of violent convulsions from which, while
the great mass of the people groaned in bondage,
the country was never free. Both these causes were,
however, in full operation fifty years before emancipation came to pass. It is therefore manifest that there
must have been a third cause, a cause even more
pressing than the other two, and which inclined the
balance in favour of freedom.

This cause is not far to seek. Every manual of
political economy tells us, and experience proves,
that in every country where slavery prevails there
arrives a time when it ceases to profit individuals,
and becomes prejudicial to the best interests of

the State. When food is dear a slave, whose heart
can never be in his work, may consume as much as
he produces, and so earn little if anything for his
master; and industrial development is altogether
incompatible with involuntary servitude. Hence the
enfranchisement of Russian serfs was not alone a
question of humanity, it had become an economic
necessity. During what may be called the prepa-
ratory period, from 1855 to 1860, when the Crimean
War had made manifest the misery and backwardness of Russia, in comparison with other countries,
the most effective arguments used by the advocates
of freedom were of the economic order. And the
immense industrial development which ensued in
the sixteen or eighteen years (until, as we shall
presently see, despotism put fresh obstacles in the
way) after emancipation took place, proved to demonstration the justice of their views and the wisdom of
the measure.

In this way, and as a direct consequence of the
growth of enlightenment and the internal development of the country, the last economic burden laid
on the people by political coercion was removed.
All the functions of the national life were now performed without Government interference, simply by
the spontaneous operations of ordinary causes and
the promptings of individual needs. The knout was

no longer required to drive peasants to the fields and
craftsmen to the workshop. Public life became tran-
quil. The country ceased to be a volcano in a state
of ebullition, because for the implacable hatred felt
by the slave for his master was substituted the
relatively mild antagonism between employer and
employed.

This being the case, what need was there for an
autocracy — a military dictatorship? What need
for the Central Government to retain its absolute
authority and unlimited power if it had only to
perform simple and peaceful administrative duties
as they are performed in neighbouring countries? It
is a grotesque anomaly. The autocracy has lost
its political *raison d'être*—its right to be. It has
become useless, and consequently insupportable and
tyrannical. The instructed classes were the first to
perceive this. It was they who felt so strongly the
shame and injustice of keeping the people in bondage, and who wrought so ardently for their emancipation. How, then, could they help being moved to
indignation by the virtual slavery imposed by the
autocracy on themselves and the country at large?

It was only in the nature of things that con-
currently with the movement of 1860 in favour of
freeing the serfs, there should be a general movement
among all the instructed classes of Russian society in

favour of liberalism and all that it signifies. But the autocracy remained immoveable. Owing to the peculiar condition of the country the Government had at its disposal an immense force, and it resolved to resist to the utmost.

There are two causes which render an open struggle against the Russian absolutism extremely difficult. The first is that which, during the whole of our unhappy past, has served so well the turn of despotism —the vast size of the country, the immensity of distances, and the poverty of great centres of population —conditions that make the common concerted action of considerable masses materially impossible. The second cause (less important because less permanent, though it promises to disappear within a measurable time, and is for the present of great gravity) arises from the want of moral union among the different classes of the nation. Russia has no *bourgeoisie*, in the proper sense of the word, none like that which made the French Revolution of 1789, and provided the people with leaders and guides. Our instructed and liberal class is composed for the most part of *ci-devant* nobles and small landowners, to whom the people have not yet forgiven the wrongs they suffered at the hands of their forefathers.

Thus the Government, which keeps its forces terribly concentrated, has before it an enemy scattered and.

crushed, materially and morally disunited. The strategic position of the Government is therefore cruelly strong. It makes the most of its advantages, runs counter to the best interests of the nation, and while oppressing the still ignorant masses, wages against the instructed class a war without mercy and without truce. For twenty-five years has this contest continued, ever extending, ever developing fresh phases, and becoming ever more cruel and desperate.

In the following pages I propose to make clear the true nature of the struggle which is now going on, and the phase which it has reached. That done, we shall endeavour to present its probable result.

PART II.

DARK PLACES.

CHAPTER X.

At St. Petersburg on a night in the year 1875. The clocks have just gone two; the town is asleep, and a deep silence reigns in the capital of the Tzar. The wide and empty streets, dimly lighted with flickering gas-lamps, straight and erect like a line of soldiers, look as if they, too, were taking their repose after the fatigues and excitement of the day. The innumerable little carriages, with their diminutive horses, which form so striking a feature of the great city, converting their now deserted thoroughfares into an ever-flowing stream of wheels, horseflesh, and human heads, have vanished from the scene, and the few drivers that still remain on the stands, vainly hoping for fares, are fast asleep on their own droshkies. The *dvorniks* (porters) of great houses, having neither visitors to receive nor suspects to watch, sleep in their niche the sleep of the just, while

the hollow ring of his footsteps on the granite flagstone
reminds the solitary wayfarer of the lateness of the
hour. At the corner of Liteinaia Street and the Bas-
seinaia, a *gorodovvi* or city sergeant stands on guard.
Having to keep order in his beat, he is supposed to
be wide awake, and as he leans against a wall with
his hat pressed low on his head, it would puzzle the
sharpest of inspectors to know whether all his senses
are steeped in oblivion, or he has merely shut his
eyes the better to meditate on the world's wicked-
ness, and the most effectual methods of defeating the
wiles of perturbators of the peace. The good man
may indulge without compunction in these solitary
musings. The soothing influence of the night has
appeased for a while the passions, the greed, and the
struggles of the human ant hill around him. St.
Petersburg sleeps its first sleep, and all is quiet.

But what is that strange company which emerges
noiselessly and mysteriously from the great house
near the suspension bridge over the dark and deep
canal? One by one they come until some fifteen
are assembled in the street, whereupon, in obedience
to a whispered order, they " fall in " and glide swiftly
through the deserted streets. Half of them are clad
like common·folk, the others are in uniform. Had
the civilians marched in the centre, there could be no
doubt as to the character of the *cortège*, but the men

in mufti go in front and lead the way, the military bringing up the rear. As this strange company pass towards the Liteniaia, the tramping of their feet and the rattle of their arms seem to affright all who hear them. The slumbering gorodovvi rouses himself with a sudden start, pushes back his hat, stands bolt upright, and gives the military salute to the leader of the company, which, however, the latter does not deign to return. The droshky driver, wakening up rubs his eyes and glances in fear at the portentous apparition. The belated passenger, when he sees it, turns hastily into a by-street, and there waits until the procession has gone past; then, coming from his hiding-place, he follows the group with his gaze, wondering whither they are bound, and perchance regretting that their destined victim, less fortunate than himself, will be unable to keep out of their way.

For these men are intent on no errand of kindness or mercy. They are servants of the State, guardians and representatives of public order, on their way to vindicate the authority of the law and perform an act in its defence.

Let us follow them.

After traversing several wards, they turn into a little street on the right, and call a halt, whereupon three of their number draw aside and literally and figuratively put their heads together. Then they separate, and the owners of the heads give whispered directions to the others, pointing the while to a large house hard by. It is against this building, which contains many dwellings, and looms through the darkness like a great grey giant—the windows all closed like the eyes of a man who sleeps in security, fearing no evil—that the attack is to be made. The force divides, one slipping round the street corner to take the giant in the rear, while the other goes boldly to the front, and wakens the slumbering dvornik. The man, jumping up in sudden alarm, mutters some incoherent words, but is speedily silenced by one of the men in civil dress. Then, without question or hesitation, he lets these peremptory visitors, who may be robbers in disguise, into the house of which he is the appointed guardian, lights a lantern and, hatless and half-clad as he is, his long beard streaming in the wind, leads the way. With catlike steps, procurator, policemen, and spies mount the staircase, the gendarmes raising their sabres and treading softly, while the civilians exchange remarks in lowered voices. They might be taken for a band of brigands, led by a man whom they had forced to be their accomplice.

"It is here," says the dvornik at length, pointing to a door.

On this the leader makes a sign to his men "to hurry up," and the next moment they are all assembled before the door. After assuring himself by a rapid glance that every man is in his place, the chief whispers something in the dvornik's ear, and asks him sternly "if he understands."

The dvornik nods his head, goes to the door and gives a strong pull at the bell. This he rings a second time, and a few minutes later the sound of footsteps is heard inside.

"Who is there?" asks a woman's voice.

"It is I, Nicolas Ivanoff. I have a telegram for the master."

On this the key is heard turning in the lock, the doors open, and the crowd of *sbirris*, pushing back the half-dressed servant, swarm into the dwelling.

The vindicators of order are now in possession of the fortress. Their next proceeding is to secure the garrison. Everybody being asleep, they can only do this by going into bedrooms, heedless of the screams and protests of frightened women and the cries of suddenly awakened children.

The first surprise over, the father of the family demands of the one who seems to be the leader, who he is, and the meaning of the intrusion.

"I am the *pristav*," is the answer, "and this gentleman is the procurator. We are come to make a search."

"I have not the pleasure of knowing you. You have a warrant, I suppose?"

"Of course. Otherwise I should not be here."

"Would you be good enough to show it me?"

"It would be useless. Besides, I have not brought it with me. I left it in my office. But there can be no mistake. You are surely Mr. N——. Your daughter lives with you. She is in that bedroom. We want nothing more. It is on her account we are here."

"But you will at least send your men out of the rooms. My wife and daughter cannot dress in their presence."

"They will have to do so, though," says the police officer, with a grim smile. "Do you think I am going to leave them unwatched? They might conceal or destroy something that could be used as evidence against them."

The father, after a further remonstrance, finding himself altogether powerless to hinder the threatened outrage, asks that his protest may be recorded in the protocol.

"Certainly, if you wish it," says the officer, with a contemptuous gesture. "But what difference will that make?"

The mother and her young daughter are then made to rise from their beds and dress before the men, who have taken possession of their room. If the commander of a search party in these circumstances withdraws his men for a few minutes from the room, it is an act of pure courtesy and complaisance on his part. The law and his superiors allow him to do as he thinks fit.

At length all the members of the household are up and clothed. Every adult is then given in charge to a policeman—one to each. Another officer is told off to watch over the children, and prevent them from communicating with their elders, and the search begins. First the chambers are overhauled, bedclothes turned topsy-turvy, drawers opened, their contents tumbled on the floor, and everything minutely examined. The next proceeding is to search the attic rooms, for not a hole or corner of the dwelling is overlooked. Books, papers, and private letters—especially the last—are eagerly sought and carefully inspected. Nothing is sacred to Russian police agents. The young lady who has incurred their suspicion, and given them all this trouble, watches their doings unmoved, as it would seem, in full assurance that the search will lead to no compromising revelation. But unfortunately for her this confidence proves to be premature. A policeman opens the drawer of a little

cabinet in which she keeps her own particular letters,
and as he fumbles amongst them she perceives a bit
of paper whose existence she had forgotten. The
sight of this morsel of manuscript moves her to the
quick ; she becomes painfully agitated ; for though
there is nothing in it to hurt her, it contains a name
and an address which may be the means of delivering
another to imprisonment and exile ; and the fault
will be hers ! After a cursory glance at the paper,
the officer lays it aside and goes on with his inspection of her letters, a proceeding which suggests to
the poor girl a desperate expedient. With a single
bound she is at the cabinet, and, seizing the paper,
puts it into her mouth. But the very same moment
two brutal hands are at her throat. With a cry of
indignation the father rushes forward to protect his
child. In vain ! before he can reach her he is pushed
back, forced into a chair, and held there fast, while
three of the ruffians deal with the young girl. One
holds her hands, another grasps her throat, and the
third, forcibly opening her mouth, thrusts into it his
dirty fingers to get out the paper which she is trying
to swallow. Writhing, panting, and desperate, she
does her utmost to accomplish her purpose ; but the
odds against her are too great. After a short struggle
the *zerbere* lays on the table a piece of white pulp,
streaked with blood, and as the men loose their hold,
their victim falls fainting on the floor.

"The insolent conduct," as it is called, of Miss N—— will be fully set forth in the official depositions.*

Whether the address which Miss N—— desired to destroy be deciphered or not will now make very little difference to her personally. The mere attempt will be taken as proof of conscious guilt and punishment meted out to her accordingly.

The search is now conducted with greater zeal than ever. Many of the letters are read at once, others are taken to be read at leisure. Everything in the house is necessarily, in these circumstances, at the mercy of the police—plate, jewellery, cash, all pass through their hands—and it is an open secret that the victims of a search often lose both liberty and money, or money's worth. Yet complaints are rarely made, and for very good reason. Even if the thief could be identified, a most improbable contingency, restitution would almost certainly be refused, and the man who attacks the police makes for himself a host of implacable enemies, who are sure sooner or later to have their revenge.

The search goes on until daylight. Every corner

---

* The scene above described is no imaginary one. It happened thus to Miss Varvara Battushkoff, daughter of General Nicolas Battushkoff. The police, in trying to force a piece of paper from her mouth, broke one of her teeth, and many more young girls have been similarly maltreated.

has been examined; even the chair cushions have
been ripped open, and the flooring of the young lady's
bedroom taken up, on the chance of finding beneath
it some forbidden books or compromising papers.
For, as all English readers may not be aware, the
possession of literature which the State deems per-
nicious is in Russia a penal offence.

The business is now over and the tragic moment
has arrived. The young lady is sternly bidden
to say farewell to her kindred. No tears are shed,
they are too proud, too indignant to show such weakness in the presence of the enemy. Yet in the out-
wardly calm countenances of the parents, as they
fold their child in their arms, may be read a very
agony of apprehension and sorrow. What will become of her? Will they let her out alive? Shall
they ever see their darling again? It may be with
her as with others. . . . With a desperate effort the
mother keeps down a rising sob—her heart is torn
with anguish—she kisses her child again, perhaps
for the last time; the prisoner, too much overcome
to speak, tears herself away and hastens to the door.

Five minutes later is heard the rolling of the wheels
which convey the lost one to the dungeons of the
Tzar; and a darkness, as of night, has descended on
these three lives, it may be for years, it may be for
ever. One is that of a young creature now doomed

to unknown sufferings, but yesterday full of energy and life; two others are those of parents long past their prime, whose secret tears and silent grief are all the more bitter and intense that they have neither the martyr's courage nor the hero's hope.

CHAPTER XI.

THE kind of search I have described, known in continental countries as a "perquisition" (albeit in most of them no domiciliary visit can be made in the night), but for which the English language has no equivalent, because no English-speaking people have the thing, though it may be regarded as the ordinary and normal Russian method, is not the only one, being modified according to circumstances and the caprice of those by whom it is conducted.

From time immemorial Russian police searches have been made by night—deeds of this sort loving darkness rather than light; but it would be wrong to infer therefrom that Russian families enjoy absolute immunity from these unwelcome visitations during the day. The police often make searches during the day, because it is the time when they are least expected, when people are the least prepared to receive

and, possibly, to deceive them. They like to take
their victims by surprise, and they know that a man
whom they want generally leaves his friend's, house
towards midnight and repairs to some undiscoverable
hiding-place. A secret meeting will adjourn rather
than continue its deliberations until a late and, therefore, a dangerous hour. As the police, by appear-
ing unexpectedly, may a make rich prize, they do not
restrict their visits to any particular time. On the
other hand, there are good reasons why they should
make them mostly at night. In the first place,
nocturnal searches cause less scandal than daylight
visits. All that the neighbours know next morning
is that somebody has disappeared. At one or two
o'clock a.m., moreover, the police are pretty sure to
find people at home and to take them more or less by
surprise. Hence the watches of the night, when, in
other countries, the sanctity of the home enjoys the
special protection of the law, is of all others the time
when the subjects of the Tzar enjoy the least security
and are exposed to the gravest perils. During the
periods of "white terror," which generally follow on
great attempts or detected plots, when searches by the
hundred are made right and left, there is hardly a
family belonging to the educated classes who, on re-
tiring to rest, do not tremble at the thought that
before morning they may be roused from their sleep

by the despot's emissaries. At one of these periods
(after the Solovieff attempt), the ordinary gaols being
so crowded with prisoners seriously compromised that
there was no room for the many persons who were
merely suspected, without a shadow of evidence, the
latter had to be confined in the common room of
Litovsky Castle. They lived together and were very
gay, as in Russia is always the case when many
friends meet unexpectedly in prison. Before going
to bed, as one who was there has told me, they would
say to each other, "Ah, we shall sleep soundly to-
night, for here we are in safety"—a grim pleasantry
of which none but those who have lived "under the
Tzars" can understand the full significance.

Deceiving people by a falsehood or a stratagem in
order to make them open a door without mistrust is a
common proceeding of the Russian police. When
(on December 16, 1878) they wanted to arrest Dou-
brovkin, an officer quartered at Starai-Russa, a town
not far from St. Petersburg, they caused the chief
of his battalion to say that he had an important communication to make to him on the business of the
regiment. The police of Odessa, desiring on one
occasion to make an arrest, raised a cry of fire at the
door of their victim, who, rushing out in all haste,
only half clad, fell into their hands and was carried
off without ceremony. But when searches are so

frequent that everybody expects them, the police, as a rule, reserve their artifices for special cases. For as an engineer may be hoist with his own petard, so may an artifice be turned against its contrivers. That of the telegram brought by a dvornik in the dead of night is becoming somewhat stale, and when an alarm of fire, or of any other calamity, is given you scent a still greater danger and forthwith burn your papers and otherwise prepare yourself for an imminent police visitation.

Your arrangements completed, you open the door and play the part of an ingenuous innocent. The police cannot well punish you for not making haste to receive an apocryphal despatch, or to escape from an imaginary fire. Knowing this, they mostly prefer to knock loud enough to awaken the dead, crying at the same time, " The police! the police! open the door or we will break it in."

Nor is the threat a vain one. The Russian police make no scruple about housebreaking, an art in which they are as accomplished as professional burglars. They sometimes begin in this way—when they can do so without making a noise. At the seizure of the clandestine printing-office of the *Tcherny Peredel* (on January, 1880) the gendarmes, either by lifting the doors from their hinges, as the official report said, or by using skeleton keys, as ran the rumour,

took the inmates by surprise and arrested them all
as they lay in bed.

Violence and brutality were always in Russia the
concomitants of domiciliary searches and arrests, and
with the increase of severity in the treatment of
political criminals generally, the violence has become
greater and the brutality more ruthless.

What causes, it may be asked, are held sufficient
to justify the defenders of order in making these
nocturnal visitations and troubling so cruelly the
repose of peaceful citizens? The question is one
which occurs naturally to an Englishman, but if put
to a Russian he would merely shrug his shoulders,
and smile at the simplicity of the observation.
"Could anything be more absurd!" he would probably exclaim; for in Russia it is a question of the
zeal of the police, never of the rights of the subject.
Russia is in a condition of internal warfare, and the
police, being the right arm of one of the belligerent
parties, does not protect, it fights. Wherever the
enemy is they must be ready to attack him; any
place where he is supposed to be they must beset.
An officer of police who hesitates to make a search
without sufficient cause, or an arrest without a
warrant, would be looked upon as not worth his salt,
an idler who wanted to receive fat pay without giving
anything in return. A member of the force who

desires to win promotion or even to keep his place cannot afford to be scrupulous. He must be as keen, as vigilant, and as ready as a sleuth-hound on the quest. At the least sign, or the merest suspicion of a scent, he must join in the chase and seize the quarry, where he can. And come what may, let the sign be ever so deceptive, the chase ever so fatal, he is always encouraged by the thought that he will merit the approbation of his superiors. For never yet has it happened for an officer of police to be punished for making a search on insufficient grounds. I doubt if for this cause a reprimand has ever been given, and it is quite certain that the men who have the fewest scruples are the most rapidly advanced.

Here are a few instances—by no means extreme—of the methods of our Russian police, taken almost at random from the great mass of materials at my disposal:

On a fine day in May, 1879, a small army composed of infantry, Cossacks, and gendarmes set out from the town of Koupiansk, province of Karkoff, drums beating, music playing, drum-major at their head, and muskets at the trail as if they were marching to meet an invader. But the force being under the command of the procurator it was evident that the enemies they were about to encounter were either actual rebels or suspected Nihilists. The first object of attack was Mr. Boguslavsky, a large landowner. The garden and grounds were surrounded by a cordon of soldiers, while the procurator Metchnikoff, at the head of a posse of policemen and gendarmes, beset the house, which naturally surrendered at discretion. After turning everything upside down in their usual fashion, they examined the garden with equal care, dragged the fishpond, and left no corner of the premises unvisited. But their search was fruitless, and they had to go away as empty-handed as they came. Nevertheless Mr. Boguslavsky was placed under domiciliary arrest, and a guard left in possession of his house.

The detachment next paid a visit to Mr. Balavinsky, justice of the peace for the district of Senkoff, whom they treated in like manner, but, as before, the police discovered not a shred of evidence to justify their suspicions. Were searched also the houses and grounds of Mr. Voronez and Mr. Dihokovsky, rich landowners who had filled public offices, with the same result. Nothing was found. Nevertheless Mr. Voronez was taken away to prison, and, after being kept for some time in custody, exiled to a remote province in the north, that of Olonez. What he had done to merit this punishment he never knew. It was said at the time that there had been some rumours to his disadvantage among the peasants.

At length the procurator withdrew his men and took his departure, leaving the representatives of the Koupiansk nobility in a state of utter bewilderment as to the cause of the sudden and unwelcome visit they had received, and the annoyance to which they had been exposed. Nor had they yet done with this zealous official. A few months later he paid them still another visit, proceeded precisely in the same way as before with precisely the same result. But as it was deemed necessary to show some wool for all this cry several innocent persons were arrested and exiled by administrative order ; for, on the principle that guilt should not be imputed until it is proved, we have a right to assume that the very fact of these unfortunates being neither brought to trial nor accused of specific offence implies their innocence.

With Mr. Kotchalovsky, justice of the peace for the district of Ekaterinoslav, the procurator was more fortunate. The police found in his house the manuscript copy of a speech delivered by a workman called Peter Alexeeff, at the "Trial of the Fifty." For this crime the judge was exiled to Archangelesk, in the extreme north of Russia.

Until it was revealed by the indiscretion of one of his clerks, the case of the procurator's excessive zeal remained a mystery. In 1874, that is to say five years previously, Mr. Leo Dmokovsky, one of the

early apostles of revolution, was sentenced to eight
years' hard labour for having printed, in a clandestine
printing-office, two socialist pamphlets. But a part
only of his type and plant were taken, the rest he
had either destroyed or hidden safely away. Now,
as it happened, this gentleman was also a Koupiansk
landowner and akin to several of the neighbouring
gentry.   So Mr. Procurator Metchnikoff, turning
things over "in what he was pleased to call his
mind," came to the conclusion that the missing type
was concealed in some country house of the district.
Hence this military pomp and parade, all these portentous visits, house searchings, fish-pond draggings,
and the rest, proceedings which both surprised and
amused the peasants and other inhabitants of the
neighbourhood.

According to another version—in a country where
the press is fettered rumour naturally takes the place
of news—the procurator had some old scores to settle
with the nobility of Koupiansk, and took this means
of "serving them out," the affair of the lost type
being merely a pretext.

An equally characteristic incident came to pass in
August of the same year in the government of
Tchernigoff. Mr. F——, doctor of the district of
Borzensky, a public functionary in the service of the
Zemstvo, received a visit from Madame B——, wife

of a magistrate of Kieff, a lady of rank and a *persona grata* in the *salons* of the governor of the province. She was accompanied by a maid and a man-servant. Immediately on Madame B——'s arrival her host as in duty bound notified the fact to the local *ouriadnik*, a sort of rural constable, at the same time showing him her papers—a passport granted by her husband, the magistrate, and a certificate signed by the president of the judges of Kieff. The doctor mentioned that there were two persons in the lady's suite, but that their papers had been inadvertently left behind at Kieff, whither he proposed to telegraph for them. This, however, as Madame B—— was staying in the neighbourhood only a few days, and the doctor could personally vouch for her respectability, the *ouriadnik* declared to be unnecessary. Judge then of her surprise when three days afterwards the *pristav* (chief of police) called at the house and wanted to see her. Thinking that the man had made a mistake, that it was her host he wanted to see, she sent word by her maid that Doctor F—— was not at home. But this only led to a repetition of the demand, the *pristav* insisting that it was Madame B—— he wanted to see, and see her he would. So she went to him in no very good humour, and asked what he meant by thus importuning her. But instead of apologizing, he stigmatized her as a "suspect," and put her under domiciliary arrest. He also arrested her two servants, and led them off to the prison of Borzna.

The true and only motive for this proceeding was the desire of Kovalevsky (the *pristav*) to distinguish himself, and emulate the example of his comrade, Pristav Malakoff, whose zeal in making arrests had been rewarded by the approbation of his superiors, rapid advancement, and better pay. The reason assigned for the arrest of Madame B——— and her servants, as set forth in the official report sent to the chief of the Kieff police by the *pristav* of Borza, was that a woman had arrived there without papers, who, according to current rumour, kept a milliner's shop in the Krechtchatik (one of the principal streets of Kieff) the better to conceal her participation in revolutionary plots ; and milliners and shopmen being, as was well known, Nihilists in disguise, Madame B———'s pretended maid and man-servant, as well as their *soi-disant* mistress, were placed under arrest. A few days later, when the passports had been verified, the lady's identity established beyond doubt, and everything found in order, they were all released " without a stain on their characters;" but they received no amends for their unwarrantable detention, nor the *pristav* any reprimand for his sharp practice.

Mr. Henri Farino, member of a highly respectable French firm, being at Klinzy, a manufacturing town

in the province of Moscow, for a purely business
purpose, happened to meet at the house of his host,
a notary of the name of Szelovsky, the chief of the
local police, to whom he was presented in due form.
For some unexplained reason the latter gentleman
before leaving asked his host for the Frenchman's
passport. The document granted by the Republic,
and visé at St. Petersburg, as also by the Governor
of Moscow, was found to be unimpeachably correct.
Nevertheless Mr. Farino's luggage was overhauled,
his person searched, his money taken, his letters and
other papers carried off to be searched, and himself
placed under arrest. But the intercession of Mr.
Subzelovsky, and of Professor Isaeff of the Jaroslav
Lyceum, procured his provisional release, and a few
days later the French Consul obtained from the
central authorities an order for the restoration of his
countryman's effects, and his full discharge.

With such instances as these volumes might be
filled. It will be observed that in every case which I
have adduced, the initiative was taken by the police.
The cases in which the police are set in movement by
the denunciation of private enemies and amateur
informers, are, if possible, still more numerous and
revolting. Creatures, the vilest and most abject, the
very offscourings of society, who would not be believed
on their oaths, have it in their power, by secret accu-

sations and pretended revelations, either to gratify
spite begotten of envy, or avenge imaginary wrongs
on the objects of their hate. No denunciation, by
whomsoever made, remains innocuous. A cook whom
you have dismissed, or a thieving man-servant whom
you have threatened to prosecute, has only to say you
are a Socialist, and the nocturnal search follows as a
matter of course. Is there a competitor who annoys
you, a former friend to whom you want to do an ill
turn?—you have only to denounce him to the police.
When the Government, in a lucid interval, instituted
the so-called Committee of Revision, they were shocked
by the number of false denunciations that came to
light; yet which, despite their fraudulent character,
had been most disastrous for their victims. It was said
at the time that the minister would prosecute these
perjurers and false witnesses. But the times changed.
The reaction set in, and under the *régime* of Count
Tolstoi, every hope of reform was abandoned, every
good resolution forgotten, and the crowd of spies and
denouncers were allowed to resume their dirty work.

Informers are not even obliged to give their names.
An anonymous denunciation has just the same effect
as a duly signed charge. It sets the police to work.
The domiciliary visit and the midnight search follow
as a matter of course. Subsequent proceedings
depend on the discovery of compromising documents,

or of facts which the leader of the search party may deem suspicious.

The police are respecters neither of numbers nor persons. There is a house in Cavalregarde Street, St. Petersburg, not far from the Tavreda Gardens, which occupies nearly a whole quarter. It is a building of five storeys, contains scores of small dwellings, and is probably inhabited by at least a thousand persons. Many of the inmates are medical students, attached to the Nicolas Hospital hard by. The heads of the police heard a vague rumour that, somewhere in this rabbit warren, dangerous people were in hiding, and, possibly, subversive plots being hatched. A nocturnal visitation was promptly organized. At dead of night the vast building, big as a cotton factory, was beset with a battalion of infantry and an equal force of policemen. The latter, broken up into detachments of threes and fours, swarmed into the corridors, the staircases and the stair-landings. They made incursions right and left; a dozen inmates were summoned "to open to the police" at the same time. The alarm spread like wildfire; in a few minutes everybody in the house was awake and afoot, and lights gleamed in all the windows. But a sentinel posted at every door kept the inmates prisoners until their turns should come. The dwellings were searched in batches of twelve at a time, by as many different search parties, and the inquisition went on until every part of the building had been thoroughly overhauled. Nothing whatever was found; but the police, not liking to go away empty-handed, carried off several captives, all of whom were released a few days afterwards.

This is far from being a solitary case. After great "attempts," above all, after the first and the last, it was seriously proposed to search every dwelling in St. Petersburg. This, of course, could not be done—the thing was physically impossible—but several streets were actually overhauled from house to house, and from end to end. One block of buildings at a time was surrounded by a regiment of soldiers who arrested and detained every one who tried to enter in or go out. While this went on outside, the police were at work inside. When they had done, they went to the next block, and repeated the operation until the whole street had been gone through.

These marchings of soldiers at dead of night, this breaking like burglars into the dwellings of peaceful citizens, rifling their rooms and terrifying their children, seems to have been conceived in the very wantonness of despotism. The system was equally scandalous and absurd. The searches were useless; the searchers found nothing, for their visits being expected—sometimes mysteriously announced beforehand—measures were always taken to render them abortive. Sudeikin understood this. After his advent to power they were discontinued, for one reason, perhaps, because since that time there has been no great " attempt." Yet none the less is the fact of the system having existed, and been so rigorously practised, highly characteristic of the methods of Russian government, and the views of those who rule on the important principle known as " inviolability of the domicile." Judged by the in- fallible test of their actions, they deem the sanctity of a man's home, the quiet of his house, to be utterly unworthy of respect. Police on the quest are no more expected to give heed to the trouble and harm they may inflict on peaceful citizens than the hunter, hot in chase, is expected to give heed to the grass on which he tramples, or the brambles which he thrusts aside.

Another extraordinary incident of the system of search, as practised in Russia, is that, as the right of domiciliary visitation belongs to sundry functionaries, who act independently of each other, several descents —two, three, and even four—are sometimes made on the same house in the same day. This, though hardly credible, is strictly true. In the spring of 1881, there was staying at Clarens, on the shores on Lake Leman, a Russian lady, the widow of Councillor

R——. She was then about forty years old, and had four children. During the panic that followed the 13th of March, this lady received seven police visits within the space of twenty-four hours. Seven times in one day and night did she hear the terrible summons, "Open to the police;" seven times was her house ransacked, and herself compelled to undergo a cruel ordeal.

"This was more than I could stand," she said. "I have four children; so I left St. Petersburg and came here."

It may be thought that this lady was deeply and notoriously compromised, or, that at any rate, the police had strong ground for suspecting her of complicity to some revolutionary enterprise. Not the least in the world. In that case she would have been promptly arrested. She was innocence itself, and so void of offence that when she wanted a passport for Switzerland, the police made no difficulty about complying with her request. The seven searches were made at random, "by pure misunderstanding," as was afterwards explained. Misunderstandings of this sort are frequent in Russia. It has befallen only too many to be arrested by mistake, exiled by a misunderstanding, and kept several years in prison under a misapprehension. All this has happened. I shall say more thereupon in a future chapter. It is a fact well known to every Russian; and when the police limit themselves to making unwelcome visits, and searching our houses by night, we consider ourselves fortunate in being let off so easily.

The position of Russian subjects with reference to the inviolability of their domiciles, is aptly described in a scene by our great satirist.

" Do you know what it would be necessary to do, to satisfy everybody? " asked Glousnov of his friend.

" It would be necessary to have two keys for every house. One I should take for myself, the other I should give to the police, so that they might come in whenever they chose to satisfy themselves as to my innocence. Would it not be equally advantageous for both sides? "

The friend sees the matter in precisely the same light; the proposed arrangement, he thinks, would be a great advantage for everybody concerned. But he gravely reminds Glousnov, that in most houses there are a strong box and a plate chest, that his project might possibly expose him to the suspicion of desiring to tempt the guardians of order to " lay hands on the sacred vessels." That would be serious!

CHAPTER XII.

BUT let us return to our heroine, whom we left on her way to prison under the escort of a brace of gendarmes.

From the corner of the vehicle in which she is ensconced she can see over the closed blinds into the street where, early as it is, people are beginning to move about. The poor girl seems quiet and resigned, but her eye dwells on every object she passes as if she might never see it again, and despite her outward composure her brain is working with feverish activity. In half an hour, perhaps in a few minutes, the prison doors will be closed upon her. She will have to undergo an examination. That is certain. But of what will she be accused—what can the police have against her? And as the carriage rattles over the stony pavement, her eyes still fixed on external objects, she turns her mental gaze inward, and examines herself before the tribunal of her own conscience. She is only eighteen years old, and has lived at St. Petersburg—where she came to pursue her studies—but a few months. Not a long time, yet long enough for her to have committed several high crimes and misdemeanours, poor child! First of all she is on terms of close friendship with a certain X, once a student, now an ardent and successful revolutionary propagandist among the peasantry. He was the companion of her childhood. When they were in the country he sometimes wrote to her, and it was one of his letters which she had tried to destroy. At St. Petersburg they met as occasion served, and through his introduction she had made several new acquaintances of like views with himself. One was Miss Z——, to whom she was indebted for many acts of thoughtful kindness, and to whom she rendered several in return. Once, when the former anticipated a visitation from the police, she took into her charge a packet of forbidden books. Another time she took a pamphlet to a fellow student, and, last of all, she had allowed Miss Z—— to use her address for the former's correspondence. Serious offences all of them, and if the police knew everything she would be utterly lost! But they could not know everything. Impossible! Yet something they must know—or suspect. How much, and what? That was the question.

Here our captive's reverie is interrupted by the sudden stoppage of the carriage, and looking through the window she sees a fine four-storied building in a style of architecture at once elegant and severe. It is the palace of the new inquisition—the House of Preventitive Detention. How well she knows the hypocritical building with its long ranges of high and beautifully arched windows, hiding, like the serried squares of soldiers at an execution, the horrors going on within! How often had she stopped before the double-faced building, thinking with a mingled sense of admiration and sorrow of the unfortunates who languished behind those pretty semi-rustic walls! Who could have thought that in so short a time their fate would be hers! She alights, and with a grave, preoccupied face approaches a tall, majestic gateway, like that of some beautiful temple, just high enough to admit the car of the condemned, who are prepared for their last journey in the prison yard. A wicket in the massive brown door silently opens, and the sentinel, a great giant of a man who handles his big musket as easily as if it were a bamboo cane, gives no more heed than the stone posts that border the footpath. Then there is a rattle of bolts behind her; the wicket closes. Who can tell when it will open again—for her?

They take her to the office; they put down her

name, age, and description. Then a voice cries from below :

"Receive number (let us say) thirty-nine!"

"Ready!" answers a voice from above.

Number thirty-nine, escorted by a warder, mounts the staircase. On one of the landings she is delivered to another warder who conducts her to cell thirty-nine.

This cell is thenceforth the captive's world. A little box, but new, clean and neatly arranged, four paces wide and five long. A truckle-bed, a little table fastened to the wall, a little stool, a gas-pipe and a water-pipe. She examines all these objects with curiosity and a sense of pleasant surprise. After all, the devil is not so black as he is painted. She has hardly finished her examination when she is startled by strange noises—mysterious rappings coming, as it would seem, from the inside of the wall. Placing her ear to it she listens intently. The knocks, though weak, are distinct. They do not come regularly and mechanically, but with a rhythm and cadence as if they were inspired by an intelligence, and were meant to convey some hidden or spiritual meaning. What could be the import of the mysterious sounds? Ah, she understood! She has heard say that the inmates of prisons sometimes communicate with each other by means of little

knocks—after the manner of a telegraphic alphabet.
These rappings must come from a neighbour—some
companion in misfortune who wishes to speak to her.
So in token of thanks and sympathy she gives back
a few answering knocks. The next moment, to her
utter surprise, there are rappings all round her.
From the opposite wall comes a series of sharp loud
knocks as if the knocker were boiling over with im-
patience or anger. There was then another fellow
sufferer in need of sympathy! As she raises her
hand to reply there comes a sound from below as
rhythmic, yet more sonorous than the others. The
medium in this case is the water-pipe, and then, as
if it had been an echo, comes a similar call from
above. The little box is filled with these little
sounds, as if crickets were at work, or as if the
mysterious beings believed in by spiritualists were
rapping messages from the invisible world.

The captive's first feeling was one of fear. Were
there, then, prisoners above her, prisoners below
her, prisoners on every side of her in this sinister
abode? Was she but a solitary unit in a swarm
of unfortunates? Then came a sense of annoyance, of keen regret, that it had never occurred
to her to learn this prison alphabet. Her inability
to understand the rappings which continued to re-
sound in her cell made her ashamed of herself—

almost desperate. What could they mean? What were her unseen neighbours saying? Not knowing the interpretation she could answer nothing. One by one the knocks ceased, and the same profound silence as before reigned around her. But a few moments later one of the knockers began afresh. Perhaps he pitied the new comer's ignorance, and was offering to instruct her. This time the knocks are lighter and more distinct, as if to enable her the better to count them, and are not, as previously, so interrupted by pauses. As she listens, strenuously trying to make out what they can mean, she has a happy thought. It is that each knock may correspond with a letter of the alphabet according to the order in which it is given. In that case the reading of the rappings will be an easy task. She will wait for the first pause, and when the knocks recommence link them with letters of the alphabet— one for the first letter, two for the second, and so on. The pause comes. It is followed by more knocks. Listening eagerly, and counting with rapt attention, she makes out a letter, then another, then a third. The three form a word. Then two more words are spelled out. "Who are you?" asks her neighbour.

"How shall she answer?" In the same manner of course. So she telegraphs her name, and a few other phrases are exchanged. Her obliging neigh-

bour next teaches her the code, equally simple and
convenient, by means of which, after a little practice,
conversation becomes easy and rapid.

It is through this acoustic language that hundreds
of intelligent and sensitive beings, though invisible
to each other, and for ever divided, exchange ideas
and commune together. Deprived by the implacable
cruelty of their fellow men of human society, condemned to live and suffer in a silence as of death,
it is to the walls that shut them in—dumb witnesses of their solitude—that they communicate their
musings and tell their griefs. And the stones and
the iron, more compassionate than men, transmit
their thoughts to others equally unfortunate. When
detected the rappers are severely punished for these
infractions of the rule which condemns them to un-
broken silence. Yet the walls, kind, faithful friends
—accomplices who never betray—are always there
inviting them again to beguile their solitude and dis-
burden their griefs by converse with their unseen
companions.

But it is not possible to punish every violator of the
rule of silence; the black dungeon would not hold
them all, and the offenders are so numerous that the
authorities are compelled to wink at the offence.
There is no prison of the Tzar in which communication by knockings does not prevail, and it is more

prevalent in the House of Preventitive Detention than in any other.

Number Thirty-nine is quickly familiarised with the strange and original life of her prison-house, and forms fast friendships with people whose existence is revealed to her only by the rhythmic rappings on the wall. But community in suffering and similarity of disposition take the place of less abstract relations, and ties are sometimes formed in captivity which last a lifetime. It is said that love laughs at locksmiths; he laughs also at gaolers, and people have been known to fall in love through the medium of prison walls. Number Thirty-nine is an apt scholar, and shares to the full in the sentiments, the ideas, and the enthusiasm of the new world, which the Tzar's police have discovered for her. Never before has the young girl lived so full a life. Occupied almost exclusively with her studies, she has felt hitherto for the cause of liberty but a silent sympathy, accompanied by ideas more or less vague. Now she understands everything. She has heard of the sufferings and sounded the souls of the prisoners around her. She sees how devoted they are, how faithful and ardent; and now, full of the zeal of proselytism, she rejoices in the thought that she also is strong to suffer and to do.

Yet she is sad withal, for the life histories of

her invisible brothers and sisters have been unfolded to her, and they are dark with suffering and sorrow. They belong to every order, from the merely suspected to undoubted rebels and notorious propagandists.

Number Forty, her next-door neighbour, is seriously compromised. He was taken in *flagrante delicto*, disguised as a peasant, provided with a false passport, and carrying on an active revolutionary propaganda. He was a rich landowner and magistrate, and will certainly be condemned to a long term of penal servitude. Sixty-eight can hope for no milder punishment. A young woman of high culture and noble birth, she finished her studies at the University of Zurich; then, returning to Russia, she took a place as factory-girl in a Moscow cotton mill. Arrested on suspicion of being a revolutionary emissary, several contraband pamphlets were found in her box, and a workman was frightened by the police into confessing that he had heard her read one of them aloud to some of his comrades. No very heinous offence, it may be thought, yet quite enough to ensure conviction and, probably, a long term of penal servitude. These, however, are among the more fortunate. They know the fate in store for them, an advantage denied to many of their companions. Nineteen, in the cell below, for instance, is accused of nothing in particular. The

pamphlet seized by the police was really too frivo-
lous to make its possession an offence. But on the
pretext that he was a friend of Number Forty they
have kept him in prison two years and a half. The
charge against Sixty-three is equally trivial. He
once made a visit to the estate of a propagandist,
since convicted. But not one of the peasants with
whom he was confronted could testify anything against
him. Yet the procurator was " persuaded in his own
mind " of Sixty-three's guilt, and this is the latter's
third year in prison.* Though quite a young man,
confinement has seriously impaired his health. Number Twenty-one, on the upper storey, is even worse.
He suffers from phthisis, and the deadly disease is
making rapid progress. He was on friendly terms
with a celebrated propagandist, and attended several
private Socialist meetings, where politics formed the
subject of discussion. For two years he has been in
daily expectation of release. But when he leaves his
narrow cell it will be for the still narrower confines of
the tomb, that last and sure refuge of the oppressed.†
All night through she hears the stricken man's hollow
cough, and her heart is full of pity and sorrow.

But her neighbour of the right gave her yet keener

---

* A fact. This is precisely the case of Nicolas Morozoff (arrested
1873 at Tver).

† Equally a fact. The victim in this case was Voinoiasezky.

pain, even more than pain—horror and dismay. This neighbour was one of her own sex; and so rapid and strange—incoherent even—were her rappings, that it was some time before Thirty-nine could understand them.

"Distrust Forty," she said, "he is a spy. So is Twenty-one. They are put there expressly to surprise our secrets. They come into my cell when I am asleep at nights. They put a pipe into my ear, and pump up all my thoughts to show them to the procurator."

The woman was mad. The charge against her was preaching the gospel of Socialism. Like Sixty-three she got work in a cotton mill and played the part of a factory-girl. A few days later, and before she had time to commit any breach of the law, she was arrested. But the fact of her disguise was regarded as proof of her guilt. Eighteen months' solitary confinement turned her brain, but they still kept her in seclusion. And from all parts of the vast prison-house the rhythmic rappings on the wall brought equally heartrending stories of suffering and sorrow.

CHAPTER XIII.

POOR THIRTY-NINE.

AND the examination ? And the interrogation ? Why
have I forgotten the main point, and relegated the
secondary to the first place ? my readers will probably
ask.

Because in Russia juridic procedure is not the main
point. It is secondary and accessory. The chief
point is to secure the prisoner, to keep him in
" durance vile." As for trying him, examining the
proofs against him, determining his innocence or his
guilt, these are things about which there is no hurry
—they can wait.

Here is a case in point, perfectly authentic and
susceptible of fullest proof, which affords an excellent
example of Russian judicial methods. In 1874 Mr.
Ponomareff, a student in the Saratov seminary,
was taken into custody on a charge of belonging to a
secret society. Among the papers of one of the

leaders of the movement, P. Voinaralski, had been found a ticket on which was written Ponomareff's name. This was held to be a sufficient justification of his arrest. At the interrogatory the latter denied all knowledge of the former, saying that he had not the least idea how Voinaralski became acquainted with his name. Persisting in this denial he was accused of obstinacy, urged to confess, and still proving recalcitrant, sent to prison and advised to "reflect." As he reflected there three years, it cannot be said that the authorities did not give him ample time to consider both sides of the question. Similar instances of obstinacy are far from rare among political prisoners. But the richest part of the affair—the point of the story—did not come to pass until 1877, when Ponomareff, at length placed on his trial, retained Mr. Stassoff, a well-known St. Petersburg advocate, for his defence. The advocate, naturally enough, asked to see the *pièce de conviction*, the ticket on which his client's name was affirmed to be written. The ticket was produced accordingly, when, lo and behold! the name was not the name of Ponomareff at all. Owing to a slight similarity in the spelling of their cognomens the notice had mistaken him for somebody else, and arrested the wrong man! So lax is the administration of the law, so cynically indifferent are the dispensers of the Tzar's justice to the rights of the Tzar's subjects, that it took three years—the time allowed Ponomareff for reflection—to rectify an error that in any other country would have been rectified within twenty-four hours.

But let us take up the thread of our story.

The very day of her arrest Thirty-nine was taken before the procurator, from whom she learnt that the visits she had occasionally made to X. were known to the police; and his letters, which the latter had seized, showed that their relations were of a somewhat friendly character. The suspicions already conceived—suspicions which had suggested the nocturnal search—were confirmed by the attempt of Thirty-nine to destroy her friend's letter. Than this, she found to her great relief, nothing more was known. All the same, she was roundly accused of belonging to the secret society directed by X., a society having for its object " the overthrow of the existing order, subversion of property, religion, and the family," and so forth. These charges she naturally denied. She was accused of other offences, and many searching questions were put touching her supposed connection with the revolutionary movement. All were answered in the negative.

" Very well," said the procurator at length, " you will have to reflect. Take Number Thirty-nine back to her cell, warder."

Thirty-nine went back to her cell, rejoicing that she had come so well out of the ordeal, and that the police had so little against her. Her spirits rose, and she was full of hope as to the future.

She was allowed to reflect at her ease; she could not complain that the even tenour of her thoughts was disturbed by too many distractions. A whole week passed, a second, a third. An entire month elapsed, and still nothing was said about another examination. The month multiplied by three, by four, by six. Half a year went by without any break in the monotony of her life, a life passed within the four walls of her little box, from which she emerged but once a day for a few minutes' lonely walk in another box, differing from the first only in being open to the sky—a compartment of the court divided into squares, each enclosed within high walls for the use of prisoners kept in solitary confinement. No wonder the poor girl began to be somewhat weary with the insupportable sameness of her existence; and wonder, not without anxiety, what would be the end.

But towards the end of the seventh month, when she has almost abandoned hope, she is called before the procurator to undergo still another questioning. Surely they will let her go now!

At any rate, they did not keep her long in suspense. The examination was brief and sharp.

" Have you reflected ? "

" Yes, I have reflected."

" Have you anything to add to your previous depositions ? "

" Nothing."

" Indeed ! Go back to your cell, then. I will make you rot there."

" I will make you rot there." This is the stereotyped expression; an expression which few political prisoners have not repeatedly heard.

Thirty-nine does not this time return to her cell with a light heart and a beaming countenance, as she had done after her first interrogatory. She feels crushed and confused, weighed down by a strange, almost agonizing sense of apprehension and despair, which at first she is unable either to define to herself or to understand. What can it be? whence came it? Ah, that snake of a procurator ! And then she remembers the words with which he had dismissed her to her cell. He would let her rot there ! And there were proofs all round her that he did not threaten in vain.

The maniac in number thirty-eight is knocking furiously at the wall.

" Wretched traitress, you have been to denounce me. Here is a man with a sack of hungry rats that he is bringing to devour me. Coward, coward, that you are ! "

The poor lunatic is in one of her paroxysms.

A horrible fear takes possession of the prisoner's mind.

" Dreadful! dreadful! " she cries; " shall I one day become like her?"

The months go and come, as if time and memory were not; the seasons follow in their unvarying round. It was autumn when she lost her liberty, then another autumn came and went, and now a third is passing away—yet freedom returns not; it seems as far off as ever. Poor Thirty-nine still languishes in her cell, so woefully changed by confinement and solitude that even her own mother would hardly know her.

At the end of her second year of prison the captive underwent a terrible crisis. Her wretched life within the four walls of the diminutive cell, the frightful sameness—no change, no occupation, no society, no anything—became utterly intolerable. The yearning for air, movement, liberty, grew intense, almost to mania. On waking in a morning she felt that unless she was released that very day she would die. And she had nothing before her but prison — always prison!

She bombarded the procurator with letters, entreating him to order her into exile, to send her to Siberian mines, to sentence her to penal servitude. She would go anywhere or do anything to escape from her living tomb.

The procurator came several times to her cell.

" Have you anything to add to your depositions ? " was his invariable question on these occasions. " No ? Very well, I must still leave you to your reflections."

She begged her mother to try to get her enlarged on bail, pending her trial. But her parents could in no way help her. All their applications received the same response : " Your daughter is obstinately im-penitent. Advise her to think better of it. We can do nothing for you."

She fell into utter despair. Dark ideas of suicide began to haunt her brain. More than once she thought she was going mad. From these calamities her physical weakness, by lessening the intensity of her life and numbing her susceptibility to suffering, alone saved her. (This is why in Russian prisons the young and vigorous succumb the soonest. The feeble and delicate have a better chance.)

Want of air and exercise, and insufficient and un-suitable food, have produced their natural effect on that young and undeveloped organism. The bloom of health has long since vanished from those cheeks, once so fresh and fair. Her complexion has as-sumed that yellow-green tint peculiar to sickly plants and to the young who linger long in captivity.

But she is not thin; on the contrary, her face is swollen and puffy, the result of softening of the tissues, produced by seclusion and inaction. All her movements are slow, indolent, and automatic. She looks six years older. She can remain half an hour in the same position, with her eyes fixed on the same object, as if she were buried in deep thought. But she is not, for her brain has become as flabby as her muscles. At first she read greedily all the books which the prison authorities allowed her mother to bring her. Now, however, she finds concentration of thought so difficult that she cannot read two consecutive pages without extreme fatigue. She passes the greater part of her time in a state of torpor, in heavy drowsiness, moral and physical. She has no desire to talk or lay plans. What can it profit to talk to the air, to speak of the future when you are without hope? The early friends of her imprisonment, the kindly and responsive walls to whom she had once imparted her innermost thoughts, are almost abandoned. She rarely goes near them. And the walls themselves, with the delicacy of true friendship, understand her silence and respect her sorrow and despair. From time to time they speak softly words of consolation. But receiving no answer they desist, lest they should annoy her with what, in her hopeless condition, might seem like mocking phrases. Yet they ceased not to think of her and to watch over her with loving care.

"It is not well with Thirty-nine," said one wall to another.

From wall to wall, from stone to stone, the evil tidings run, and the entire building vibrates sadly in response—

"Something must be done for poor Thirty-nine."

The voice of the stones at last finds expression in human voices. The prisoners beg the warders to send a doctor to Thirty-nine.

The prayer is heard and the doctor comes, accompanied by a policeman. Thirty-nine is examined. It is quite an ordinary case—prison anemia. The lungs are severely affected; the nervous system is thoroughly deranged. In a word, she is suffering from prison sickness.

This physician was young at his business as a gaol doctor. He had some humanitarian ideas, and his heart was open to pity. But he was so accustomed to the sight of suffering that he could contemplate it unmoved. To show over-much compassion for a political prisoner, moreover, might expose him to the suspicion of being a secret sympathizer with the disaffected.

"There is nothing serious the matter," said the man of physic.

The stones learnt the verdict in mournful silence. Oh, how terrible are the sufferings, how unutterable the sorrows, these walls have witnessed! But they can still feel, and when the doom is pronounced they sigh : "Poor Thirty-nine! What will become of poor Thirty-nine?"

Yes, what will become of poor Thirty-nine? Oh, there are many alternatives for her, all equally possible. If by some shock her vital energy should be awakened and the acute crisis return, she may strangle herself with a pocket handkerchief or a piece of linen, like Kroutikoff; or poison herself, like Stransky; cut her throat with a pair of scissors, like Zapolsky, or, in default of other means, with a bit of broken glass, as Leontovitch did at Moscow, and Bogomoloff in the Preventitive prison of St. Petersburg. She may go mad, like Betia Kamenskaia, who was kept in prison long after her lunacy had declared itself, and only released when her condition was utterly desperate, to poison herself shortly afterwards in a fit of suicidal mania. If she continues to fade she will die of phthisis, like Lvoff, Trutkovsky, Lermontoff, and dozens of others. Relenting too late, her custodians may release her provisionally, but only to let her die outside the prison, as they did with Ustugeaninoff, Tchernischeff, Nokoff, Mahaeff, and many others, all of whom fell victims to phthisis a few days after they were provisionally enlarged. If, however, by reason of abnormal strength of character, vigour of constitution, or other exceptional circumstances, she should survive until the day of trial, her judges, out of consideration for her tender age and long imprisonment, may let her end her days in Siberia.

All these eventualities are equally possible for Thirty-nine. Which will come to pass none can tell. The fates must decide. For as I propose in this book to say nothing doubtful or uncertain, I will hazard no conjectures as to the issue. So let us drop the curtain and say farewell to Number Thirty-nine.

CHAPTER XIV.

As I have just observed, it is impossible to foretell categorically the fate in store for any individual prisoner of the Tzar. Yet, by making a calculation of probabilities, according to the rules admitted by statistical science and based on indisputable facts, we may form a fairly accurate idea of what is likely to befall any of these unfortunates in whom we may happen to take an interest.

In the trial of the 193—one of the principal trials of the period in question—the imperial procurator Gelechovskij said, in his requisition, that of the entire number there were no more than twenty who deserved punishment. Nevertheless, of the 193 accused persons no fewer than seventy-three committed suicide and went mad during the four years that the examination lasted. Hence, almost four times as many as the public prosecutor himself

deemed worthy of punishment were either killed by
inches or visited with a doom more terrible than
death.

The 193, moreover, did not include all on whom
the police laid hands and brought before the tribunal.
The arrests and imprisonments in connection with
the trial were at least seven times greater, reaching
a total 1400, of whom, however, 700 were set free
after a few weeks' or a few months' detention. The
other 700 were kept under lock and key for periods
varying from one year to four years, and appeared at the trial either as principals or witnesses,
the latter being of course the more numerous. The
senate, by whom the 193 were tried, pronounced two
different sets of sentences—the one nominal, and of
extreme severity, the other milder, real, and intending,
in the form of a recommendation to mercy, to be
laid before the Tzar and by him sanctioned and
confirmed. One was sentenced to penal servitude, 24
were sentenced to exile in Siberia, 15 to simple exile,
and 153 were acquitted. I call the latter the real
sentences, because recommendations to mercy, above
all, when coming from an exceptional tribunal composed of high magistrates, are, as a rule, never
refused by the Emperor. But, less merciful than
his own judges, Alexander declined to act on their
recommendation, and ordered the sentences, passed

by the senate in the belief that they would not be enforced, to be carried out in all their rigour. These sentences—thirteen of the 193 only being sentenced to penal servitude—amounted in the aggregate to seventy years' penal servitude, the heaviest penalty—inflicted in one case alone—being ten years' penal servitude. *

Now if we reckon, on the other hand, but two years of preliminary detention for each of the 700 persons originally implicated in the prosecution—and this is decidedly below the mark—we get a total of 1400 years—fourteen centuries of a punishment far more fatal to its victims than the penal servitude of Siberia.

Thus the pains inflicted by the police were twenty times greater, for the same offence, than the penalties imposed by the tribunal, albeit the latter went to the utmost limit allowed by the draconian code of Russia. In other words, to obtain evidence for the conviction of one man, the same punishment meted out to him was inflicted on nineteen innocent persons. This, without taking into account the seventy-three unfortunates that died during the examination, and whose deaths in at least seventy

---

* Exclusive of the 700 who were released in the course of the first year, and taking no account either of the twenty sentences of police supervision inflicted by the tribunal, or of the sentences to exile afterwards inflicted by the police.

instances were directly traceable to the effects of their preventitive detention, passed, be it remembered, in the solitary, soul-destroying confinement which either maddens or kills. That these seventy-three persons were nearly every one virtually murdered is proved by the fact that, according to a calculation based on the mean mortality of St. Petersburg, and taking into consideration their ages, only two or three of them ought to have died during the period in question.

Such are the methods of the Russian Inquisition.

CHAPTER XV.

THE QUESTION.

THE system described in the foregoing chapter may be called the slow and quiet system. The "impenitent" are left to rot peaceably in their cells, in the expectation that these fruits of official zeal, which are still green, will after a period of rotting become more pervious to the inquisitors' pincers, and admit of the extraction of their hidden grains.

Yet, despite its evident advantages, this system has one great drawback. It requires time and patience. So long as Nihilists did not go from words to acts, and limited their proceedings to a peaceful propaganda, there was no need for hurry. The agitation was not feared. From time to time suspected propagandists were caught here and there, and, after putting them in prison, their captors awaited with folded arms in the generally vain hope of revelations which might enable them to get up a monster indictment for conspiracy.

But when the revolutionists, weary of merely passive resistance, took up arms and gave back blow for blow, the authorities could temporize no longer. With a view to guard against the terrible reprisals which the police had reason to believe were being prepared by the Nihilists outside, the police deemed it imperative to obtain from the prisoners the fullest information in the shortest possible time. In these circumstances, the slow process of letting prisoners rot until one or other might think fit to reveal did not answer. To obtain prompt results it was needful to intensify their sufferings. From this necessity the police did not shrink. The rigours of preventitive detention were augmented. With cruel craft they struck first at the most sensitive point. The isolation of the prisoners was made absolute and complete. Every indulgence was withdrawn; it became the isolation of the tomb. The House of Detention, with its comparatively mild discipline, was reserved for prisoners the least compromised. Serious cases were relegated to that vast and gloomy fortress, where the police can work their will on their victims, unchecked and unseen. In towns so fortunate as not to possess a sufficiency of suitable dungeons, temporary lock-ups were improvised. Political prisoners were hindered from communicating with each other by placing common gaol birds in the intervening cells.

Their places were sometimes taken by gendarmes and spies, who, knowing the language of the walls, acted as eavesdroppers, and even as *agents provocateurs*. No means were spared to break the spirits of impenitent suspects and render their lives intolerable. They could neither write nor receive letters, were forbidden to see their friends, and deprived of pens, paper, and books, a deprivation which to an intellectually active man is alone dire torture. On the other hand, signs of yielding were warmly encouraged, and on the pusillanimous who made depositions favours were showered with lavish hands.

The cruelties inflicted on the obstinate—and most of the prisoners were obstinate—gave rise to a frightful struggle, the so-called strike by famine. Having no other means of asserting their rights against their relentless oppressors, the prisoners refused to eat. In some instances they went without food seven, eight, and even ten days, until they were on the verge of death, when the police, afraid of losing their victims altogether, would promise concession, such as the privilege of reading and writing, taking their daily walk in common, and the rest—promises, however, which were often shamelessly broken. Olga Lioubatovich had to refuse food for seven consecutive days before she could obtain a needle and thread wherewith to vary the monotony of her life with some womanly work.

There is not a prison in which hunger-strikes have not taken place three or four times.

But the method of examination is that into which the most subtle refinements have been introduced. Beforetime the resources of the inquisitors were limited to somewhat remote threats—Siberian exile, hard labour in dismal mines, solitary confinement, indefinite preliminary detention — penalties severe enough, in all conscience, yet, as was thought, not sufficiently striking in their effect on the imagination. Now it is very different. The Tzar's procurator can hold before the eyes of his prisoner the spectre of the gallows. He tries to compel confessions by threats of death, which are much more terrifying than threats of transportation and penal servitude. The horror of capital punishment for puerile offences lends peculiar efficacy to this method of extorting admissions.

"You know that I can hang you," Strelnikoff was in the habit of saying to his victims. "The military tribunal will do whatever I direct."

The prisoner knew it only too well.

"Very well, then," would continue the public prosecutor, "confess, or in a week you will be hanged like a dog."

Falsehood and perfidy were likewise resorted to without scruple.

"So you won't peach. Very well; you are determined to sacrifice yourself in order to save men who have admitted their guilt and betrayed you into the bargain. Read this."

Whereupon the inquisitor would show the prisoner a counterfeit deposition—counterfeit from beginning to end, with bogus signatures and forged evidence—containing all the things which Strelnikoff wanted the prisoner to confess.

He practised at times other and, if possible, still more cruel devices. After letting a young husband catch a glimpse of his wife, also a prisoner, pale, worn, and sick, he would say—

"You have only to cease your useless denials, and both of you shall be set at liberty."

There were occasions on which this Torquemada of despotism would blend cruelty, deception, and lying in a cynical and ingenious combination.

"I do not want to harm you. I am a father myself. I have a young daughter like you," he said to Miss P——, in Kieff, in 1881. "I am touched by your youth. Let me save you from certain death."

The young girl still refused to confess.

On this Strelnikoff had her father led in, an old grey-haired man, devotedly attached to his daughter, and described to him in highly coloured language the peril of her position, and the terrible charges that hung over her head.

" She will die, die ignominiously in the flower of her youth," he exclaimed. " Nothing but confession and sincere repentance can save her. But I am powerless to move her. You try. Beg of her, implore her—on your knees, if necessary."

And the poor old man, distracted with terror, sinks weeping before his child, and beseeches her not to bring his grey hairs with sorrow to the grave ; and the child, shutting her eyes that she may not behold the terrible sight, tries to flee.

Though tragical enough for the victims, this was a pure comedy contrived by Strelnikoff, who had not in his possession a shred of evidence against Miss P——; a stratagem to draw from her damaging admissions.

A man who is not very clever, especially a young man, may easily fall into one of these perfidiously laid traps, and let a word or a detail more than he intended inadvertently escape him. So soon as the mistake is perceived, it becomes a cause of burning remorse. It may be a mere bagatelle, a nothing. But that matters not; the overwrought imagination, with its monstrous exaggerations and fantastic apprehensions of possible consequences, makes everything to the worst. The mind of the unhappy prisoner is haunted by the fear that he has ruined his friends and betrayed his cause. We must read the autobiography of Khudiakoff, a pure-minded and honest man, who behaved with the greatest firmness in the Karakosoff trial, if we would understand the hell that such an apprehension as this may create for a sensitive and conscientious nature. Nothing can compare with suffering so horrible, self-torture so intense—suffering, moreover, which, on account of the complete isolation of the prisoner, may last for months. In the deadly loneliness to which he is doomed there is no kindly soul to offer him a word of consolation, no thoughtful friend to point out the insignificance of the mistake which he has committed.

It may, without exaggeration, be affirmed that the ravages wrought of late years among Russian political prisoners are due even more to their infamous method of juridic procedure than to the cruel system of preventive detention, the brutality of gaolers, or the privations to which their victims are exposed.

Strelnikoff is the general type of the modern inquisitor, albeit the type necessarily varies according to the predominance of one or other of the characteristics of which it is composed. Paniutin, once aide-de-camp to Mouravieff the hangman, afterwards the right hand of Todleben, hangman of the Souths, is the type of the ferocious inquisitor. The leading features of his methods were violence and brutality. "I may have to hang five hundred and exile five thousand, but I will purge the city." These were his very words.

The celebrated Soudeikin—who was so well known that I need say no more about him—is the refined inquisitor of the Judas type, the type most prevalent at St. Petersburg, and whom the highest dignitaries are not ashamed to take sometimes as their model.

For instance, the Dictator Loris Melikoff presented himself in person to prisoners condemned to death, the day after trial, and under threat of confirming the sentence, and with the rope almost literally in his hands, demanded names and betrayals. Yet the General had in his possession commutations of their sentences signed by the Emperor.

I will not bewilder and shock my readers with further description of the different species of this family of reptiles. I shall only observe in conclusion that the judicial code of Russia, repeating the codes of neighbouring countries, runs thus: "The object of preliminary detention is to prevent the accused from evading examination and judgment." Another paragraph of the same code interdicts the use of "threats, cajolries, promises, and all other like means for prevailing on the accused to give evidence." And it is further laid down that in the event of the examining judge having recourse to such means the depositions shall be null and void.

This, as will be seen, is the very antithesis of the practice with regard to political prosecutions. Here the system of the inquisition is in full force. The Government having decided that avowals and revelations are necessary for its own protection, stops at nothing to obtain them. In its eagerness for useful information, it neither heeds the sufferings of the innocent nor respects the laws itself has ordained. The examination designed for the furtherance of justice has become a system of moral torture and physical pain; and preventitive detention an expedient for rendering it impossible for suspected persons to escape these new substitutes for the thumbscrew and the rack.

CHAPTER XVI.

POLITICAL TRIALS.

"But we must finish, my dear sir. We cannot let a preliminary examination last ten years. It will become a scandal. Foreign papers are beginning to make a noise about it. The Emperor is dissatisfied. Do the best you can, but in any case see that your requisition is ready at the latest in two months."

These words were addressed by the minister to the public procurator at an early stage of the revolutionary movement.

A little later a general—satrap of his district—spoke as follows:

"The Court is quite furious about the last attempt of these cursed Nihilists. We must let them see that we mean to have an eye for an eye. Fudge a trial for two weeks hence. We must strike the iron while it is hot."

And the procurator, fired by ambition and a wish

to be well thought of in high quarters, did "get up" a trial. The merit of a public prosecutor, it may be well to explain, is always estimated by the magnitude of his prosecutions and the complexity of the plots which he discovers and exposes. It seldom happens, however, that in cases of supposed conspiracy the procurator can obtain sufficient evidence to convict justly those whom he suspects and has decided to arraign. But that matters little. He treats conjectures as certainties, suspicions as evidence, personal friendships as proofs of affiliation, visits of courtesy as proofs of complicity in the supposed plot. In a word, the trial is "fudged up." It is sometimes not unlike a game of cross purposes and crooked answers. People who have never met in their lives before are accused of belonging to the same secret society, the offence of one person is attributed to another; a man is charged with instigating an act which he did his best to prevent. But these are trifling errors, unworthy of serious attention. The indictment was drawn at haphazard and by fits and starts. The main point is that a sufficient number of persons, supposed to be implicated in the same diabolical conspiracy, having been got together they can be tried in common.

And the tribunal before which they are brought, what is it, how does it work? English readers of a judicial turn of mind may be desirous of knowing how a court for the trial of political offences is composed in Russia. I will try to satisfy them, but before doing so I must observe that it is merely a question of curiosity, and that the subject possesses no more than an academic interest. In a country like Russia, where the authorities can do absolutely what they please with a man, after as well as before judgment, the way in which trials are conducted becomes a matter of secondary importance. If the history of Russian political tribunals be really worthy of attention, it is as showing the character of the Government, as an illustration of its pusillanimity, of its lack of confidence in its own functionaries, and, still more, of the contemptuous disregard which, at the slightest awakening of its suspicious timidity, it displays for the miserable thing that in Russia bears the name of law.

The Nechaeff case (September, 1871), the first after the promulgation of the new judicial regulations, was the only one tried—not by a jury, that the Government could not think of, but by the regular courts, before magistrates of the Crown performing judicial functions under ordinary conditions. It was, moreover, the only political trial as to which the privileges allowed by the law of publicity were not more restrained than is usual. The court-house was open to the public as in other trials, and the papers were permitted to publish reports of the proceedings, under the general conditions imposed by the censorship of the Press.

This unfortunate case was not of the class which appeals to the sympathy either of society or of youth. The tribunal did not err on the side of leniency, but it acquitted those of the accused against whom there was really no evidence, and it treated them with too much consideration, allowed them too much liberty in the conduct of their defence. Moreover the president, in addressing, after the verdict, the prisoners whose guilt had not been proven, reminded these reprobates that, being acquitted, they were now in the same position as all other honest citizens. Mr. Katkoff, albeit he was then far from being all that he has since become, protested that this was the prostitution of justice and the perversion of power. The Minister of Justice, Count Pahlen, was beside himself with rage, and a few months later (1872) appeared a "law" withdrawing political cases from the jurisdiction of the ordinary tribunals and placing at the same time considerable restrictions on reports of political trials. It was ordained that political cases should henceforth be judged by special tribunals, created for the purpose under the designation of Particular Senatorial Chambers. A number of senators, named by the Emperor, *ad hoc*, formed the nucleus. That the constitution of the new court might not be too bureaucratic, there were added to it so-called representatives of the three orders—nobility, third estate, and peasants. These representatives were chosen by the Government for each trial from among the marshals of the nobility, the mayors of towns, and the *starschina* (managers) of rural communes throughout the empire. On the first trial which took place after the introduction of the new law, there sat with the three senators the marshal of the nobility of Tchernigoff, the mayor of Odessa, and the *starschina* of Gatschino. Thus, in order to find three representatives to whom he could commit this delicate charge, the lynx-eyed Minister was constrained to search the entire region between the Euxine and the Baltic. The upshot showed that Count Pahlen had not laboured in vain. He made a choice which did credit to his discernment. The so-called representatives of the three orders represented, in reality, nothing but the Minister's wishes. Their docility was admirable. The representative of the peasantry distinguished himself by a zeal which might be called excessive. When the witnesses had been heard and the pleadings were finished, the six judges retired to their consulting-room, Mr. Peters, the president, requested this gentleman, as the junior member of the hierarchic order, to say what sentence, in his opinion, should be passed on the delinquents.

In every instance the worthy man gave the same answer :

" Hulks. Give them all the hulks." On this the president suggested that, as the accused were not all equally guilty, it would not be right to visit every one of them with the same punishment.

But the *starschina* of Gatschino was quite impervious to such fine drawn distinctions.

" Give them all penal servitude, your excellency," repeated the improvised judge, " all of them. Have I not sworn to decide impartially ? " *

The minister, it must be admitted, could not have made a better choice. Even he, the exacting Count Pahlen, was satisfied ; so much so, indeed, that he relegated the next trial to the same representatives, except, I believe, to him of the nobility for whom somebody still more pliable was substituted. But it is an incontestable fact that the *starschina* of Gatschino and the mayor of Odessa retained their positions and continued to exercise their judicial functions for a considerable time.

With a tribunal of this sort there could be neither difficulty nor apprehension of difficulty. It not

---

* This is authentic.

alone conformed to positive injunctions, but listened with bated breath to the veriest whisper from above. All depended on the Minister's good pleasure. When the reactionary current was in full force the sentences were of an atrocious severity. When it slackened somewhat, and the alarm at Court abated, the tribunal became more indulgent. I can, however, recall but one instance of the latter mood having any practical result; and even Mr. Peters and his worthy colleagues made, to use an expressive colloquialism, "a bad shot."

The incident came to pass shortly after the return of Alexander II. from the Turkish war. According to common report his Majesty had seen so many proofs of devotion on the part of young Nihilists, some of whom acted as nurses in the hospitals, others, fresh from the medical schools, as assistant surgeons, that he was deeply moved. He had, it was said, completely changed his views concerning the youthful enthusiasts who had been described to him by his courtiers as monsters of iniquity. The judges were therefore all for indulgence. But it was precisely at this time that the memorable trial of the 193 took place, and, anticipating, as they thought, their master's wishes, the dispensers of imperial justice gave him the opportunity of exercising the prerogative of mercy in the way I have already mentioned.   Unfortunately, however, an accident altogether unforeseen marred the finely calculated scheme of the courtly tribunal.   On the very day after the declaration of the verdict, Trepoff—who, during six months had remained unpunished for his shameful treatment of Bogoliuboff, whom he had flogged for not doffing his hat—met with his deserts.   Vera Zassoulich's pistol-shot not alone startled Europe, but changed in an instant, and to an extent almost incomprehensible, all the Emperor's ideas about young Nihilism, and converted his good intentions into bitterest anger.   Instead of a gracious smile Pahlen received a terrible reprimand, which he transmitted in due course to the dismayed senators, and their recommendations to mercy, as the reader is aware, were contemptuously disregarded.

On another occasion — the trial of the fifty (March, 1877)—it was the Government itself that did not stand to their guns.   The sentences in this case were neither under nor over the limit fixed by the law for the crime of propagandism—from five to nine years' penal servitude.   Among the prisoners most hardly dealt with were several young girls from eighteen to twenty years old, belonging to the best families of Russia.   For these ladies wide-spread sympathy was felt, even among their enemies. Most of them had studied science in Swiss universities, and they might have had a brilliant career as physicians, but fired with revolutionary ideas, they returned to their native country, there to take part in the movement. But a seemingly insurmountable obstacle hindered the accomplishment of their wishes —the deep distrust felt by the lately enfranchised people for all who belonged, really or apparently, to the same class as their former masters. Then in their burning enthusiasm these young girls resolved to renounce all the refinements of life and take upon their delicate shoulders the very same burdens which were crushing women trained to hard work. They became common mill hands, wrought fifteen hours a day in Moscow cotton factories, endured cold, hunger, and dirt, and submitted uncomplainingly to all the hardships of a sordid lot, in order that they might preach the new gospel as sisters and friends, not as superiors.

There was something profoundly touching, something that recalled the times of primitive Christianity, in this apostolate. The public present at the trial, among whom were several high dignitaries and ladies of the court, were deeply impressed, and the authorities deemed it expedient to commute the ferocious sentences passed on these young girls (whose worst offence was reading a few Socialist pamphlets to their fellow-workers), to perpetual exile in Siberia. This indulgence was not, however, extended to their companions of the other sex. Danovitch, Dgebodari, Prince Zizianov, Peter Alekseeff, whose offences were precisely the same, were compelled to undergo penal servitude in all its rigour and in its cruellest form.

Except in these two cases the tribunal and the Government have had the courage of their convictions. On no other occasion have they shown "the quality of mercy." Every act of propagandism is punished by penal servitude. And this propagandism, it should be remembered, resembles only very remotely that which is known by the same name in other countries. It does not mean the vast and sustained activity of a German, a French, or an English political movement. The conditions of Russian life do not admit of open agitation. The propaganda has to be conducted secretly in private houses and informal meetings. In the great majority of cases, moreover, the propagandist, unless he be a man of extraordinary ability, follows his arduous calling only a very short time before he falls into the hands of the police. As was proved at their trial, Dolgtshinzi printed but two pamphlets, and to neither of them were brought home more than two or three cases of propagandism. The only act proved against Gamoff was giving a couple of pamphlets to two factory operatives, an act for which he was awarded the terrible sentence of eight years' penal servitude. Those convicted in the trial of the fifty were not more fortunate. Sophia Bardina, though one of the most deeply implicated, was found guilty of nothing more serious than reading, on two or three occasions, revolutionary pamphlets to an audience of factory folks, yet for this trifling offence the tribunal condemned her to nine years' penal servitude—afterwards commuted by special favour of the Tzar to lifelong exile in Siberia.

Prosecutions of single individuals, when there can be no question of conspiracy or the organization of a secret society, and the charge is therefore limited to simple propagandism, almost always result in sentences equally severe. In September, 1877, Marie Boutovskaia, accused of giving one book to a workman, was awarded seven years' hard labour. Malinovsky, a working man, convicted of propagandism, was sentenced by the tribunal to ten years' penal servitude. Diakoff and Siriakoff, who, though tried together, had no accomplices, received the same punishment for a like offence.

Thus the utterance of a few words in favour of social or political reform is visited with precisely the same punishment—ten years' penal servitude—as that which the comparatively mild criminal code of

Russia awards for premeditated murder (unaccompanied by aggravating circumstances), and for highway robbery with violence, provided violence does not result in death.

CHAPTER XVII.

MILITARY TRIBUNALS.

SUCH was the way in which political trials were conducted in Russia during the propagandist period, corresponding with the first five or six years of the revolutionary movement.

When the attacks on Government servants began, which marked the opening of the Terrorist period, the Government promptly repeated the existing law and abolished that strange judicial machine, the famous Senatorial Chamber. Why this was done, why the worthy gentlemen who composed the tribunal were deemed unworthy of confidence, it is not easy to guess. It was so docile and obedient, so well in hand, and its high-sounding designation, the character imputed to it of "representing the three orders," were all in its favour. People at a distance might easily take this simulacrum of a court of justice for a genuine tribunal, and deem it worthy of its pretentious title. It is true that after the disappearance of the Senatorial Chamber the Government was no longer satisfied with sentences of penal servitude. Resolved to answer the red terror with the white, it demanded the gallows, always the gallows. But why not have required this from Mr. Peters? The spirited senator would certainly not have refused, and the honest *starschina* would doubtless have cried, " Give them all the rope," as he formerly cried, " Give them all penal servitude." And the courtly and cultured Mr. Novo-selski, the mayor of Odessa, would probably have answered that he was too well bred to differ from his Excellency. If the highly improbable contingency of these gentlemen professing scruples of conscience, or showing some sense of humanity, had come to pass, the Government could easily have replaced them with instruments who would stop at nothing. It is really impossible to suggest any plausible reason for the withdrawal of political cases from the competence of the civil courts, unless it was the hope that Nihilists would be terrified by the formidable spec-tacle of courts-martial, a hope, however, which could only have been realized if the Nihilists had reposed some confidence in the previous tribunal. But the fact being altogether the reverse, the conclusion was self-evident.

But the point is of little importance. Whatever

may have been the motives of the Government, the
fact remains that after August 9, 1878, a certain
category of political offenders, and after April 5, 1879
—when Russia was divided into six satrapies under
military dictators—political offenders of every sort
were tried exclusively by officers of the army, the
only class in the country whom the authorities considered competent to exercise judicial functions.* The
part of Minister of Justice was taken by generals and
other military dignitaries in high command.

But he is no good captain who, having to operate
against an enemy, follows in the track of common
routine. A good captain possesses the faculty of
adaptability; he knows how to conform to local conditions and the varying phases of a campaign.
Nothing is more natural than that our valiant
generals, transformed into satraps, and being called
upon to combat Nihilism, should act on the same
principle of sound military tactics. The present
political jurisdiction lacks the uniformity of the time
of Pahlen, who, like a true German, had a passion
for method, regularity, and rule. The composition
of the courts varies according to the taste, the caprice,
and the ideas of the different generals by whom they

---

* Only two trials out of sixty-one—that of the tzaricides, on 13th
March, and of Solovieff—were judged by the High Court, another
special tribunal.

are ordered. The normal military tribunal is composed of officers of various grades, divided into two
categories. The president and two acolytes are permanent members of the court. The others are selected
for each session from among officers of the line. The
governors-general sometimes let the court remain
unchanged. Sometimes they vary its *personnel* by
replacing a portion of the members with other officers
named *ad hoc*. Prisoners are allowed counsel, only
the latter must be military officers who are candidates for juridic functions, and officially subordinate
to the procurator as to their own chief. At Kieff
prisoners cannot be defended by civil advocates independent of the administration—although the law
permits it—and at St. Petersburg, in the prosecution
of the fourteen, permission was given to the accused
to retain regular counsel. But the latter were not
allowed access to the depositions until two hours
before the trial; and all the members of the court-
martial were named *ad hoc* by the Government.

On certain occasions, when a general desires to
strike the imaginations of friends and foes alike by
some act of extraordinary vigour, he goes straight,
and with soldierlike promptitude, to his point, equally
regardless of legal subtleties and judicial precedents.
Thus Mlodezki, who attempted the life of Loris
Melikoff, was judged, condemned, and executed on

the same day. The tribunal hardly took the trouble
to ask a question. Kaltourin and Gelvakoff, who killed
General Strelnikoff (of whom I have spoken in a
former chapter), a favourite of the Tzar, received the
same measure. Roused at dead of night, the two
men were taken to a private house, where they found
several officers, nominees of General Gourko. These,
they were told, were their judges. Fifteen minutes
later Kaltourin and Gelvakoff heard their doom, and
on the following day both were hanged.

Yet though differing somewhat in their form and
their methods of procedure, these courts are alike in
one essential point—passive obedience to the orders of
their superiors. The old judges obeyed the Ministers
as *tchinovniks* are in duty bound to do; the men
render military obedience to their commander, and
the latter would be very much surprised if they did
not. It is an incontestable fact that the sentences are
prescribed beforehand. Hence they vary, not according to the degree of a prisoner's guilt, but according
to the ideas of the governor-general of the province
where the trial takes place. We know, for instance,
beyond doubt that the sentences proposed to be passed
on the accused in the case of Drobiasgin, Maidanski,
and others (December, 1879) did not exceed deportation to Siberia, and a term or two of penal servitude.
This, in ordinary circumstances, would have been

quite sufficient to satisfy even the exigences of Russian justice, for the most seriously compromised of the prisoners had nothing worse against him than a doubtful and problematic charge of complicity in an attempt (that did not end fatally) on the life of a spy, and for which, at a later period, the principal got fourteen years' penal servitude.* But a few days before the trial Hartmann's attempt took place (December 19, 1879).

Seized by a panic, the Government resolved to make a salutary example.

General Todleben (or, probably, Paniutin) gave orders that sentence of death should be passed on the prisoners. Seeing, however, that the crime laid to their charge was neither capital nor very clearly proved, the execution of these orders, if any show of legality whatever had to be observed, was not very easy. But the tribunal was equal to the occasion. In the expedient known as "accumulative sentences" it found a way out of the difficulty. In its judgment, which may be read in all the papers of the time, there is set down opposite the name of each

---

* Leo Deutch, secretly surrendered to Russia by the Grand Duchy of Baden on the condition that he should be tried as an ordinary criminal by a civil tribunal. The promise was not kept, Deutch being tried by court-martial, which, however, in consideration of the exceptional circumstances of the case, did not pass on him an extra-legal sentence.

prisoner crimes any one of which would in ordinary circumstances have been more than adequately punished by a few years' transportation to Siberia. Then these sentences were added together, and the sum of the whole was—death! This judgment, and the tribunal's expositions of its reasons for passing the sentences in question, formed one of the most curious episodes in the annals of Russian jurisprudence.

The case of Lisogub (August, 1879) is still more extraordinary, for he neither belonged to the terrorist party nor committed any overt act whatever, either as principal or accomplice. He was a rich proprietor, whose worst offence was aiding with money the revolutionary cause. Drigo, his steward and confidant, betrayed him, and received as recompense for his treason his benefactor's considerable property. The Government, however, hoping to turn the informer's services to further account, did not expose him. Drigo neither appeared as a witness against Lisogub, nor was his evidence mentioned in the indictment. The facts were privately communicated to the judges before the trial of Paniutin, who told them at the same time that Lisogub must die. The order was obeyed, the capital sentence duly passed, and on the 10th of August, 1879, Lisogub was hanged.

Some five years ago—to be exact, on February 23, 1880—there took place at Kieff, under the rule of

General Tchertkov, the trial of a young pupil of the gymnasium, named Rosovski. While searching his room the police found a proclamation of the Executive Committee.

"Does this belong to you?" asked one of the searchers.

"Yes, it belongs to me."

"Who gave it to you?"

"That I cannot say. I am not a spy," was the answer.

In ordinary times he would have been sent to Siberia. by administrative order (without trial) ; possibly, as he was a minor (nineteen years old), he might have got off with a term of exile in one of the northern provinces. But on the fifth of the same month an attempt had been made to blow up the Winter Palace. General Tchertkov was in the same truculent mood as General Todleben. An example was needed, and young Rosovski paid with his life the penalty of other men's deeds. His sentence was death, and he died on the scaffold (5th March, 1880.)

At Kharkoff General Loris Melikoff showed every disposition to emulate the patriotic example of his colleagues. Yet although it rained political trials in other places, hardly any had taken place in his government. From April 5, 1879, when the six satrapies were created, there had been but one prosecution at Kharkoff, and even then the two principal prisoners were not Nihilists. The case, however, was a very remarkable one. Two ordinary escaped convicts, got up as gendarmes, presented themselves at the Kharkoff prison, provided with forged warrants in the name of the general of gendarmes, Kovalinski, for the delivery to them of a political prisoner called Fomin, who, as they pretended, was wanted by the examining magistrate, their idea being, of course, to effect his escape. All the papers were in order, and General Kovalinski's signature was so well imitated, that on the first blush he acknowledged it as being veritably his own. But the attempt was foiled by the treachery of a *tchinovnik*, from whom the conspirators had bought the blank warrant forms, and the counterfeit gendarmes fell into the hands of the police. But the contrivers of the enterprise were warned betimes, and got safely away. Only one of the supposed accomplices was arrested—a student named Efremoff, in whose room the plotters had met. He had, however, no idea of what they were about, had never been present at their meetings, and denied all knowledge of their doings. This was likely enough, nothing being more common than for Russian students to place their rooms at the disposal of a friend. It is, moreover, in the highest degree probable that, in order not to expose their host

to danger, the conspirators would refrain from taking
him into their confidence. Before leaving his apart-
ment they were careful to burn the paper on which
they had practised the imitation of General Kovalinski's signature. But they made a fatal omission.
It did not occur to them to scatter the charred rem-
nants with the poker; they were left in the grate in
a heap, and when the police came, and, after their
wont, examined everything, they were able to de-
cipher on a piece of paper not completely carbonized
the general's name. They showed it to Efremoff,
who, suspecting nothing, had the imprudence to read
the name aloud at the very moment the fatal frag-
ment fell asunder. This was the sole proof of
Efremoff's alleged culpability, and of his complicity
in the attempt to liberate Fomin. But a victim
being needed, he was condemned to death, and Loris
Melikoff confirmed the sentence. It was not, however, carried into effect, for Efremoff sued for the
pardon which all the others had hitherto disdainfully
refused to demand, and in consideration of his submission his sentence was commuted to twenty years'
hard labour.

These examples abundantly prove that the military
tribunals charged with the trial of political prisoners
are merely judicial purveyors for the hangman; their
duty is strictly limited to providing victims for the

scaffold and the hulks. The orders they receive they slavishly obey. Their function is to put into the shape of articles and paragraphs of the law the decrees of the administration, and give to their proceedings the sanction of a seeming legality. In the case of Kovalsky (August 2, 1878),* the first who was condemned to death, the judges, deeply moved by the speech of the advocate, Bardovski, had a moment's hesitation, asked each other how they should act, and finally resolved to demand further instruction from St. Petersburg. A dispatch was sent accordingly, and, pending the arrival of the answer—some three hours—the court reserved its decision. The answer was a decided negative, the preceding order being strictly confirmed. After this there could be no further hesitation; the death sentence was duly passed, and Kovalsky duly shot.

Did not Strelnikoff boast that the tribunals would do everything he desired? Yet, until these later times, there remained a sort of check which, though in nowise acting as a restraint on the arbitrary proceedings of the Government, imposed on its agents in ordinary cases a certain measure of decorum. This was the publicity of trials; not, however, the

---

* Although Kovalsky's trial took place before the law of August 9th, he was judged (by special order) by a court-martial.

publicity to which other European countries are accustomed, for in Russian official methods there is nearly always something equivocal, and concessions made with one hand are generally more than half taken back with the other. In order to prevent manifestations in favour of the prisoners, the audiences were sorted with particular care. Only those provided with special tickets, signed by the president of the tribunal, were allowed to be present at a trial. A certain number were given to representatives of the press, and the liberalism of the presiding judge was gauged by his generosity in this regard. But without risking instant suppression, the papers might not publish their own report of the proceedings, however guarded or insignificant it might be. They had to wait until the official text, revised, purged, and retouched by the Minister and the police was placed at their disposal. They could not print anything not contained therein, and the mutilated report had to be strictly followed.*

Access to the courts being allowed to representatives

---

* This rule gave rise to a curious custom. The official *Monitor*, having kept the press waiting an undue time for the details of a trial in which the public took great interest, the ingenious idea occurred to a paper—if I mistake not, the *St. Petersburg Messenger*— an idea afterwards acted upon by all its contemporaries, of printing, so t) speak, the outside of the trial. For several consecutive days it amused its readers with graphic descriptions of the demeanour of the

of the national press, it could not well be refused to correspondents of foreign journals, who were always both more importunate and indiscreet than their Russian *confrères*. Their telegrams, it is true, could be intercepted, and their letters seized as they passed through the post-office—sometimes; for the writers had learnt the trick of sending them by ways unknown to the police, and somehow or other the communications generally reached their destinations and appeared in print. The efforts put forth by the Government to check publicity at home and hinder the publication of unpleasant facts abroad showed how much it fretted under these practically impotent restraints on their proceedings.

Since the trial of the tzaricides (Sophia Perovskaia, Geliaboff, and others), this last remaining check—if such it could be considered—has been removed. All subsequent political trials have been conducted with closed doors. Nobody unconnected with the proceedings is permitted to be present. To this rule no exception is allowed, even in favour of the *tchinovniks* of the Tzar; for albeit these gentlemen are not

---

prisoners, their faces, the play of their features, the impression they made on the public, and a mass of other insignificant details, without letting fall a single word about the thing essential, the indictment, the evidence, and the pleadings, until the official report, having undergone the ordeal of the constabulary, was allowed to be published.

likely to have revolutionary sympathies, they might
conceivably hear something that would sap their
loyalty or corrupt their morals. At the last trial,
that of the fourteen (October, 1884), the interdict was
extended to the nearest kindred of the accused. The
public on that occasion was represented by the Ministers of War and Marine and five superior *employés* of
superhuman fidelity. So well kept was the secret,
moreover, that, according to the correspondent of the
Times, the inhabitants of the neighbouring houses
had no suspicion that a political trial was going on
in the court-house.

This, then, is our present position.

For political offences there is in Russia neither
justice nor mercy. There never has been. Ordinary
breaches of the law may be tried by a jury, but only
once has the Russian Government tried the experiment of appealing to the representatives of the
public conscience in the matter of political offences.
That was the case of Vere Zassoulitch. On this
occasion, as is well known, the authorities burnt
their fingers, and it is unlikely that the experiment
will ever be repeated. The courts have always been
the organs of the executive; they differ only in form
from the police, the gendarmery, and other branches
of the administration. All are organized on the

same arbitrary principles. The judgment, with its pomp and circumstance, is simply a dress parade, a sort of homage paid by Russian despotism to modern civilization.

And now the Government, out of mere hysterical nervousness, has little by little stripped its tribunals of every attribute which gave them the outward show of courts of justice. The present tribunals are the police, the gendarmes, the administration in all their nakednesss. I do not say that this is barbarous, or despotic, or infamous. It is simply stupid. The Russian Government may be likened to a shopkeeper who, after exposing in his window goods of seemingly fair quality, gradually replaces them with articles whose rottenness is visible to all beholders, the quality of which nobody blessed with eyes and a nose can fail to detect. I ask pardon for this unsavoury comparison, but there is really no other that fits in with the facts. The conduct of the Tzar's Government in this regard can only discredit it in the opinion of Europe without making the least impression on its enemies. For once it is decided to put a fowl in the pot, it must be a matter of supreme indifference to the victim with what sauce it will be eaten.

So far as revolutionists are concerned, the question of political jurisdiction is of the least possible

moment, and among Russians generally, it excites
little if any attention. I have dealt with the subject
because I am writing for readers to whom it is
naturally of great interest. In European countries
where the courts of justice are the supreme if not
the sole power whereby, in the last instance, the
relations between the whole body of citizens repre-
·sented by the State and each individual citizen are
regulated, the right constitution of the tribunals and
the full development of every needful guarantee for
the equity of their judgments is a matter of the
highest importance. In Russia, on the other hand,
where the police can set at naught the decision of a
judge, the constitution of the courts may interest you
as a political tribune, in that it affords you a means
of expressing openly your ideas; but in itself, as
a true court of justice—a body competent to pronounce on your fate—you cannot discuss the subject seriously. What matters it though you receive
a light sentence if on its expiration the police gives
you another far more severe? What does it profit
you to be discharged "without a stain on your
character" if the police arrest you in the very
precincts of the court, put you a second time in
prison, and send you to Siberia? What, again, is
the advantage of having your sentence of twenty
years' penal servitude commuted to one of five, if

the administration puts you in a dungeon so horrible
and noisome that, unless you are superhumanly
robust, you have not the remotest chance of out-
living even the shorter term ?

If we would learn how the Government treats its
enemies, it is not to the tribunals that we must
address ourselves ; we must know how they are
dealt with after the verdict and after the judgment.

CHAPTER XVIII.

AFTER JUDGMENT.

LET us suppose that a prisoner is condemned to the hulks for as many years as it may please the reader to give him—for truly this is a point of slightest importance, a mere matter of detail. The sentence is read with all the circumstance prescribed by the law, and the work of the court is done. Yet it is precisely at this point, when his fate is seemingly decided, that for the prisoner and those he loves arises the burning question: What will the Government do with him?

But how! And the sentence? Does Russian despotism go the length of changing at once the punishment ordered by the judges and inflicting penalties which they never contemplated? Not yet. For that there will be ample time later on. Meanwhile, the sentence is respected. But in Russia, as every one well knows, there are hulks and hulks, gaols and gaols. It makes all the difference in the world between being sent to Schlüsselburg and a Central Prison, to the ravelin of Troubetzkoi and the bagnios of Siberia.

Hence, all who take an interest in our prisoner's fate—his kinsfolk and his friends—move heaven and earth to obtain for him the unspeakable favour of being sent to Siberia. The father and mother— above all, the mother, as being the most likely to succeed in this momentous enterprise—are generally the first to make the attempt. If they are poor their son's comrades subscribe among themselves a sufficient sum to defray the parent's expenses to St. Petersburg. If, besides being poor, they are ignorant and without friends in bureaucratic spheres, they are instructed and advised—directed to appeal to some functionary whose heart is believed to be not altogether hardened, and who may, perchance, listen to their prayers and use his influence on behalf of their child. They are directed, too, to address themselves to certain tender-hearted women who, behind the scenes, have great influence in high quarters which they are often disposed to exercise in favour of an unfortunate prisoner.

Next to a mother, a wife is the intercessor whose mission of mercy is the most likely to be crowned with success. When there is no wife—and political

prisoners, being mostly young, are generally un-
married—the part of intercessor is taken by a
sweetheart. Sweethearts are never wanting. If a
prisoner has neither father nor mother, neither sister
nor brother, nor one still dearer to visit him, to
think of him, and intercede for him, his friends at
once provide him with a *fiancée*. There are few
young girls who, in such circumstances, would refuse
to play the painful and dangerous part of sweetheart
—dangerous, because acceptance of the position implies a degree of sympathy with revolutionists and
their ideas which may bring upon them the undesired
attention of the police, with all its consequences. If
the prisoner be not too seriously compromised, the
lower administration, which in these cases is the
arbiter, is good-naturedly blind to the now common
artifice, and grants the improvised sweetheart the
privilege of seeing her supposed lover, lets her take
him books and, perhaps, an occasional bottle of wine.
It is she also who, either alone or in company with
the mother, undertakes the onerous and anxious duty
of soliciting a commutation of his sentence or his
transfer to more desirable quarters.

To attain this end every possible effort is made,
every influence called into play. Mother, sister,
wife, or sweetheart, and friends, all set to work and
beseech, importune, and torment in turn procurator,

police, and gendarmery, and every person in authority whom they are suffered to approach. Refused
in one quarter they try in another; and for days,
perhaps for weeks, alternate between the pleasures
of hope and the agonies of despair. At last they
can breathe a sigh of thankfulness and relief; their
object is accomplished, their prayer granted—it has
been decided to send the prisoner, on whose behalf
so many efforts have been made, to the bagnios of
Siberia, to the land of cold and misery, of brutal
taskmasters and cruel punishments, of hard labour
in mines, where men's hands and feet are burnt by
the frozen fetters that bind them. And father and
mother, sweetheart and friends, are content withal;
they congratulate each other on their success, and
say that their beloved prisoner was born under a
lucky star!

I shall have some observations to offer further on
as to the delights which await the Benjamins of
fortune who are sent to the frozen north. Let us, in
the meantime, accompany the unlucky ones who are
consigned to one or other of the two central prisons
situate a short distance from Kharkoff, in our beautiful south, in that Ukraine which has been justly
called the Russian Italy. The first of these prisons
is in the district of Borisoglebsk, the other in the
district of Novo-Belgorod, near the village of Petche-

neghi. I shall confine my remarks to the latter, for there exist authentic documents which describe in full detail the manner of life of its inmates. These documents are two invaluable memoirs, written by two prisoners who underwent, or saw with their own eyes, all the things they have set down. One of the memoirs deals with the time before 1878, the other takes up the narrative at the point where it was abandoned by his predecessor, and brings it down to 1880. Both are of undoubted authenticity. They were written secretly, day by day, in the semi-darkness of the writers' cells, and smuggled out of the prison by one of those underground ways which, despite the vigilance of gaolers and policemen, are always to be found in the country of the Tzars. The first memoir, entitled " Buried Alive," and completed and sent away in July, 1878, was forthwith printed in the clandestine printing-office of the *Zemlia e Volia.* The second, which bore the title of " Funeral Oration on Alexander II.," left the gaol of Novo-Belgorod about the middle of 1880. It was copied and re-copied and circulated in manuscript in every important town of the empire, and a few months ago the *Messenger* of the *Narodnaia Volia* published the memoir *in extenso.*

The Central Prison is a large group of buildings, hard by the village of Petcheneghi, inclosed within a

high wall, which completely isolates them from the
rest of the living world. The uniformity of this wall
is broken by a great gateway, the only one which
gives access to this dark abode of sorrow and suffering.
On a large board above the gateway are inscribed the
words: "CENTRAL PRISON OF NOVO-BELGOROD." In
the middle of the inclosure, and about fifty paces
from the outward walls (to render escape by under-
mining more difficult) rises a vast building—the
central body of the gaol. Turning the corner of this
edifice the curious visitor, or newly arrived prisoner,
sees at the end of the court, and over against its
either angle, two single-storied houses which, though
large, are much smaller than the principal building.
Each has a gateway; on the pediment of one is
carved the inscription, " RIGHT CELLS ; " and on
that of the other, " LEFT CELLS."

These two houses are reserved for State prisoners.

Unlike the fortress of St. Peter and St. Paul, the
inmates of the Central Prison do not consist exclusively of political convicts. It is a penitentiary for
the reception of common law-breakers of the worst
type—confirmed malefactors—whom the Government
does not send to Siberia for fear they should escape.
The whole of the great central building is occupied
by convicts of this class, who form three-fourths of
the whole. Only by comparing the lot and treatment

of these two categories of prisoners can the tender care, the kind thoughtfulness of the Government for political offenders be properly appreciated.

The common criminals live and work together; minds and hands are alike occupied; they have the solace of congenial society, and, beyond the loss of liberty, have little to complain about. But their political *confrères* are doomed to complete isolation. Each man lives a lonesome life in his little cell. Even outside he is still solitary, for in order that prisoners may see as little of each other as possible, they are made to take their walks at different times and in three different yards. Attempts to exchange words with fellow-captives, casually encountered, are strictly forbidden and severely punished. No exclamation may be uttered, no voice raised in this tomb of the living.

Nevertheless, some half-dozen common malefactors are confined in as many cells of the thirty which the two houses contain. They are, of course, the greatest scoundrels of the entire collection—parricides under sentence of hard labour for life,* professional brigands, and wretches who have murdered whole families. Yet even these monsters of crime are treated more

---

* Capital punishment for other than political offences has not prevailed in Russia for more than a century, being abolished by the Empress Elisabeth in 1753.

humanely than the politicals. They are free all the day long, are allowed to work in the society of their companions, and only shut up in their cells during the night. They are neither tutored, watched, nor hindered from communicating with their fellows. Heinous as are their crimes, their yoke is easy and their burden light.

When in July, 1878, the political prisoners of Novo-Belgorod, reduced to the extremity of despair, adopted the terrible expedient of refraining from food, and began the longest and bitterest "famine strike," recorded in the mournful annals of Russian prisons, the ultimatum they presented to the governor contained but these demands :—That they might work together in the prison workshops, that they might receive food from without, and be allowed to read any books approved by the official censorship—not merely such as the governor in his caprice thought fit to select. In other words, they desired no more than to be placed on the same footing as murderers, fire-raisers, and highway robbers ; for the latter enjoyed all the privileges in question except that of reading, which, as they were utterly illiterate, they could not well have turned to account.

Yet the director of the prison, and the governor-general of the province (Prince Krapotkin, cousin of Peter Krapotkin, the prisoner of Clairvaux), let them endure the pangs of hunger for eight days (from the 3rd to the 10th of July inclusive) before acceding to these reasonable requests. It was only when the strikers were so weak that they could not rise from their beds, and every hour brought them within measurable distance of death, that, to prevent a catastrophe which would have horrified all Russia, Krapotkin yielded and promised that what they demanded should be done. But this, in the issue, proved to be a deliberate lie—a subterfuge to induce them to eat. The promise made to the ear was broken to the hope; the privileges granted to robbers and murderers were still withheld from the prisoners of state. They remained as before pariahs among outcasts.

And what, it may be asked, were the crimes of these men? Their guilt was surely great; to deserve punishment so severe, treatment so cruel, they must have been inveterate offenders—Terrorists of the deepest dye. Not at all. In a subsequent chapter I shall describe the lot of the Terrorists who were not deemed sufficiently guilty to be dealt with by the hangman. In the Central Prison were only propagandists, peaceful workers of the early dawn, the flower of the noble generation of 1870, the first that was bred and grew up in a Russia free from the stain of slavery; a generation which from the sorrowful past, pusillanimous and decrepit, inherited but a great yearning and pity for a suffering people, oppressed during centuries, and which brought to the fatherland an amount of eager devotion, a beautiful ardour, unmatched probably in any other age or country. First among these prisoners of liberty was Hypolitus Myshkin (hero of the trial of the 193), a Government stenographist and owner of a printing-office, which he devoted to the production of revolutionary literature. When brought up for trial Myshkin proved himself to be an orator of rare power. The president was utterly confounded by his apt replies and ready wit; the vast audience, one half of whom were State functionaries, hung spellbound on his lips, transformed for a moment by the magic of his eloquence into admirers and friends. His speech (November 15, 1877) was an event. On the day before, almost unknown, Myshkin, by this single achievement, became famous throughout the land. His name still lives. In the sanctuary of hundreds of solitary students, and of many a young enthusiastic girl, the portrait most often seen beside the likeness of Sophia Perovskaia is that of the intrepid young orator, with his high and noble forehead, his intellectual beauty, his large dark eyes, and his defiant bearing.

In striking contrast with Myshkin was his companion-in-arms Plotnikoff, a quiet, modest young fellow, once a student. He had not distinguished himself by any striking achievement; his political life did not last, so to speak, more than a week. Member of the Propagandist Society of the Dolgoushinzi, of which I have already spoken, he got into trouble through giving a few pamphlets to some peasants in the province of Moscow. But after his arrest his high courage and martyr-like zeal won him a lofty place even among the men ,of his circle, all of whom showed Russia a splendid example of hardihood and resolution.

"As for Plotnikoff," said the public prosecutor, in the bureaucratic language of his requisition, " albeit he has acknowledged all the crimes laid to his charge, he has not done so in any spirit of contrition, but out of pure perversity of mind; a perversity amounting to fanaticism, and excluding all hope of repentance." Better eulogy than this could hardly be made on a man devoted to a great idea.

Plotnikoff's comrade and friend, Leon Dmokhovsky, the oldest member of the Dolgoushinzi circle, was a rich landowner of the province of Kharkoff, a man of science with a heart of gold. Everywhere—in the society of his young companions as well as in the Central Prison and the hulks, where they sent him to

perish—this man was a faithful friend, a wise coun-
sellor, and, in case of need, a just arbiter for all with
whom he was brought into contact, and who required
his help. His offence was printing clandestinely,
with his own hands, two socialist pamphlets—his
sentence eight years' penal servitude.

Then there were the two sons of Kaukaze Djeba-
dori, and their adopted brother, Zdanovitch, son of
an exiled Polish father and a Circassian mother; all
three revolutionary missionaries among the workmen
of Moscow and St. Petersburg, and all three as full of
fire and spirit as the warriors of their noble country.
They were sentenced to nine years' hard labour.

Next on the roll of martyrs come Bocharoff and
Cherniavsky, two young men, one of whom was condemned to ten and the other to fifteen years' penal
servitude for taking part in the peaceful demonstration in Kazan Square.

Peter Alexeeff, another victim, was a peasant whose
bold sonorous words at his trial startled the judges,
and resounded in the hearts of his companions like a
battle call. Convicted of spreading subversive ideas
among his fellow-workmen, Alexeeff was sentenced to
ten years' penal servitude.

Donezky, Gerasimoff, Alexandroff, Elezky, Papin,
Mouravsky—their shadows, too, pass before us in this
abode of gloom. All are there. All this intelligence,

all this boundless love for the unfortunate, all their striving to raise the lot of the lowly, all are buried in that granite tomb, doomed to languish and decay.

But there are dwellers in that sinister prison house whom I have still to mention. I have said nothing of the director and chief—its right arm and moving spirit—the man Grizelevski. He displayed his peculiar talents and gained his reputation in Poland, where he was the colleague and collaborateur of Mouravieff, the hangman. He has shed the blood of Poles; he now sucks the blood of Russians. It is curious to note, by way of parenthesis, the strong predilection shown by the Government for the butchers of Poland. Panintin, Grizelevski, Kopnin (Grizelevski's destined successor), and a crowd of gaolers in Siberia, won their spurs in Poland.

Promoted by special favour of Prince Krapotkin to the lucrative and honourable post of chief of the great prison of Novo-Belgorod, Grizelevski has shown that he fully understands what is expected of him. By petty vexations without number, contrived with no other end than to torment the prisoners, and by a boundless brutality, he renders their lives a perfect hell.

Proofs and instances of his tyrannies are only too abundant.

One evening in February, 1878, Plotnikoff was

walking sadly to and fro in his little cell, reciting in a low voice some verses of his favourite poet, when the door burst suddenly open, and the director appeared on the threshold.

"How dare you recite verses!" he exclaimed with a furious gesture. "Know you not that absolute silence must reign here? I will have you put in irons."

"I have already finished my probation term,* and according to the law I can no longer be put in irons," answered the prisoner, courteously, "and the less so that I am ill: you can ask the doctor."

"Ah! you want to discuss," cried Cerberus, "very well! I will teach you the law. Bring the irons at once."

The irons were brought, the young man seized, hustled about, dragged to the office and manacled.

Another incident of the same kind (the victim in this instance being Alexandroff) befell in the month of June, 1877. Towards nightfall the song of some peasants returning from their work was heard in the distance. The song found an echo in the aching heart of the prisoner. For a moment he forgets himself and commits a dire offence—he sings. Informed of this extraordinary fact, the all-powerful

---

* A preliminary period lasting several years, during which the prisoner is treated with the greatest severity.

master hurries in person to the scene of the crime. The criminal has long been silent, and is lying on his bed—*i.e.*, on a piece of felt without covering or pillow. He gets up.

"Who allowed you to sing? Answer! Ah, you forget who and where you are! Well, I will remind you."

Before the prisoner, taken aback by this unexpected address, had time to answer a single word, the director gave him a blow on the face, accompanying the cowardly deed with a volley of oaths.

On another occasion Grizelevsky flew at Gerasimoff, formerly a student.

"What," he shouted, "you have dared to be rude to a gaoler?"

"I said nothing rude, sir," answered Gerasimoff, quietly.

"But you treated him as an equal, and he is your immediate superior, whom you are bound to venerate and respect. Do you hear? Venerate and respect. You are always to remember that you are not a man, but a convict, that you are not free, but in gaol. You have no right to expect being treated with deference. If a stick is set up before you, and you are told to bow down to it, you must do so without a word. Do not forget what I have told you, for if another time you allow yourself to be impertinent to your warder, I

will skin you from head to foot with rods. Do you
understand ? From head to foot ! "

And for what offence had the poor prisoner incurred
these brutal threats and vile insults ? Because he,
the convict, had not yet learnt to treat his warder, a
common illiterate soldier, with sufficient veneration,
and because in answer to the latter's question, " What
do you want ? " answered, " Bring * me some water,"
instead of, " Would you have the goodness to bring
me some water ? "

It might be supposed that walking being a pleasure
and not a duty, the prisoners would be free to walk
or not as they might think fit. But when the same
Gerasimoff, being rather late, and exasperated by the
brutal calls of the gaoler, refused to go out, the
director, on being informed of this act of insubordina-
tion, gave him the following paternal advice : " Why
do you not obey the gaoler ? If you are shut up—
you must remain; ordered to go out—you must
go ; if told to walk—you must walk. That is all
you have to do, and if you disobey, I'll have you
flogged."

I will not tire my readers by multiplying these
descriptions. I will only beg them to stop one mo-

---

* Speaking to him in the 2nd per. sing. *Tutoiement* of prisoners
by gaolers is universal, but the prisoner must never so address any of
the officials, not even common warders.

ment at this last cell. The inmate is an old man, and if he were not without beard and moustache and his head half shaven (as stupid and barbarous a practice as that of mutilating the face), it would be seen that his hair is grey. His hands are in gyves, he is dressed in a grey jacket, and sits near the table, absorbed in melancholy thought. And then from behind a rough voice bids him "Good-day." He rises, and slightly bowing his head, answers "Goodday, sir."

Could there be anything more polite and modest? And yet this quiet answer infuriates the foul-mouthed director.

"How dare you answer me thus, beast that you are?" he cries. "Do you forget that I am your superior?"

And this because, according to the military rule, soldiers are not allowed to answer their superior officers as men do among themselves. They have to say, "I hope you are well," adding the title of the officer. For this infraction of the rules Elezki (it is he of whom I speak) was thrown into the punishment cell. Has the English reader any idea what punishment cells in the Central Prisons are like? They are cages at the back of the *cabinets d'aisance*, and so dark and so narrow that they look, without exaggeration, like coffins—coffins, moreover, that for a man of middle height would be far too small. Prisoners cannot stand upright in them, and after a few days in this fetid hole even a strong man is seized with giddiness, is unable to stand, and seems to have passed through a serious illness.

Even when they are innocent of offence, Guzeleosky does not leave his victims in peace. Either out of pure malice, or without any motive whatever, he is always annoying and tormenting them. One day, when he was visiting the cells, he found on a prisoner's table a French exercise book himself had permitted the man to have.

"What!" he said with a cynical laugh, "you are learning French, are you? To prepare for a journey to Switzerland, I suppose?"

And he took the book away with him, thus robbing the wretched captive of a priceless solace, and depriving him of an occupation which, by exercising his mind, helped him to support the heavy burden of his solitude. If you had asked the creature why he did this—why he so harshly withdrew a favour which he had only just granted, he would have been unable to answer you, except that he so acted because it pleased him. It was a sudden caprice; he wanted to show the prisoner his power. When he is in a particularly bad humour, or things have gone wrong at home, he orders the sick to be deprived of their

beds (sick prisoners are allowed a mattress, a counterpane, and a pillow), leaving them only the felt rug,
which is the normal sleeping accommodation of the
political prisoners of Belgorod.

But, it may be urged, these are merely tyrannical
eccentricities of a brutal and ignorant soldier, de-
moralized by despotic power and left without control.
The superior administrators cannot possibly know of
these doings; if they did they would surely put a stop
to them.

Let us go a step higher, then.

The person immediately above the director is
the governor of the province. For some slight infraction of the rules the director ordered a political prisoner, affected with consumption, and who
had finished his "probation time," to be put in
irons. Exasperated by this cruelty, several of his
companions had the audacity to inform the director
that they would complain to the governor of his
brutal and unjust conduct, giving all the facts, &c.
The director could not stop a letter to his superior,
but he could punish the prisoners for writing it. So
he deprived them of books, forbade several to go out
for exercise, and shortened the exercise time for
others. Finally, he had the sky-lights in the cell-
doors, used for purposes of ventilation, closed and
nailed down. When Seriakow, who was ill, said he

could not breathe, the director expressed the wish that he might choke as quickly as possible.

But most interesting of all was the decision of·the governor. While admitting that the director had *no right to* put a prisoner who had served his probation time in irons, he nevertheless ordered him, together with *all the other prisoners* who had signed the petition, to be manacled, on the ground that they had insulted the director by their complaint; and gave them each, further, from one to three days in the black-hole!

Let us go another step higher.

In the summer of 1877, the Minister of Justice visited the prison of Belgorod in person. He entered the cell of Plotnikoff, who was almost dying, and who told him, if the horrible conditions of actual prison *régime* were not changed, all the prisoners would ere long pass from this provisional to an eternal tomb. On this, Count Pahlen, with the deliberation and German accent peculiar to him, pronounced these ferocious words : " So much the better ! Suffer ! You have done Russia much harm."

At this epoch, be it remembered, the Russian Socialists had done nothing more than distribute socialist pamphlets ! For no Terrorist, properly speaking, was ever sent to the Central Prison. The last group of political convicts for which Novo-Bel-

gorod opened its doors were the condemned of the
Kovalsky trial — Svitych, Vitashevsky, and two
others.*

With the setting in of the Terrorist period, the
position of the prisoners of Novo-Belgorod became
more and more intolerable. The Government looked
on them as hostages, and after every blow struck by
the Terrorists, discharged on their devoted heads all
the vials of its impotent rage.

"You shall pay dearly for this," said, on each
occasion, the director.

When Mezenzoff was killed, all their books were
taken away; when Krapotkin was killed, they were
put in irons; and when somebody else was killed,
all the prisoners' parents were exiled from the province of Kharkoff, and forbidden to return to their
homes. After the first attempt on the Emperor's

---

* To be quite exact, I should say that these men cannot fairly
be described as propagandists; on the other hand, they were certainly not terrorists. Though more than the one, they were less than
the other. They came to the front during the short interval between
the end of the propagandist and the beginning of the terrorist periods.
Before deciding to punish, by attacks on the agents of authority,
deeds such as those I have been describing, and preventing the infliction of further cruelties on their friends, the revolutionary party
resolved to take the defensive, and resist the police whenever the
latter sought to arrest them. This was the time when defence of the
domicile by force of arms was proclaimed as a duty. The offence of
Svitych and Vitashevsky was taking part in one of these acts of
resistance.

life, some of these unfortunates were even sent to Siberia.

Another piece of petty torture by which the prisoners were vicariously punished, was closing the ventilating orifices in their cells. In the end nearly all were closed, and they could hardly breathe. It seemed as if the director wanted to suffocate them.

In short, the system adopted in the Central Prison is substantially the same as that practised in the House of Preventitive Detention. The same isolation, the same denial of opportunity for active exercise, the same deprivation of useful work, mental and physical, followed by the same results—loss of health, phthisis, scurvy, and general bodily decay; with this difference, that prisoners awaiting their trial may cherish hopes of acquittal, and when brought up for judgment can expose the hardships they have endured, and stigmatize as they desire those by whom they were inflicted. But the others have no such consolation; hope for them is no more, protest they cannot, and complaints serve only to intensify their sufferings. Altogether at the mercy of their gaolers, they are continually vexed with brutalities and overwhelmed with insults. At the capital, moreover, prisoners under preventitive detention can communicate secretly with their friends outside, and are cheered by the expectation of meeting their enemies

face to face, as warriors are cheered when they look
forward to the day of battle. The others have none
of these advantages; cut off from human fellowship,
and oppressed with the deadly monotony of their
sombre existence, infirm in health and weakened in
mind, they have nothing to look forward to but a
life of suffering and death before the expiration of
their sentence.

I have already called attention to the effects on the
health of prisoners of the system of solitary confinement, as practised in the House of Detention.
At Novo-Belgorod, where the conditions are much less
favourable, the consequences are naturally far more
deplorable. Phthisis and typhoid fever are always
among them. If a half or three-quarters of them
still survive, their survival is in no wise due to the
care or tenderness of their custodians, who have left
nothing undone to shorten their days, but to the fine
climate and salubrious air with which nature has
blessed the Ukraine, the land of their captivity. Nevertheless, of the twenty young men in the prime of life
—their ages ranging from twenty-three to thirty—six
have gone to their long home since their incarceration in the Central Prison some four years ago. Five
died within the prison walls; the sixth (Dmokhovsky)
succumbed while being conveyed to the bagnios of
Siberia. But the most terrible scourge endured by

the victims of solitary confinement, a scourge against which favourable climatic conditions are of no avail, is insanity. At the time when the second of our chroniclers completed his memoir he says that in the right-hand cells, one of which he occupied, there were five madmen among fourteen inmates—more than a third. He gives their names—Plotnikoff, Donezky, Botcharoff, Bogoluboff, and Sokolovsky. The two first were melancholy mad ; the three others, raving lunatics, who filled the little cellular prison with fierce howlings and wild cries, heartrending sobs and maniacal laughter. Words cannot picture, the imagination is powerless to conceive, the horror of life in that bedlam for those who, though still of sound mind, are continually haunted by the fear that their stricken companions' fate will soon be theirs, and see ever before them the shadow of their coming doom. All their efforts—and, as may be supposed, they were urgent and persistent—to obtain the removal of the unfortunates to an asylum were for a long time fruitless, and never entirely succeeded. Botcharoff, one of the more violent lunatics, remained months in his cell raving mad before they took him away, and it was only after long importuning, both on the part of the doctor and the prisoners, that the director allowed him to be transferred—but not to an asylum, only to the neighbouring

central prison of Borisoglebsk, where he shortly afterwards died. As for Gamoff, they took not the least
trouble about him, and he died mad in his cell.
Plotnikoff, it is true, was removed to an asylum, but
only when his state had become so desperate that it
was evident he had not long to live, and he survived
his removal only a few weeks.

And this is not the worst. The way in which these
poor lunatics are treated by the officers of the prison
is barbarous beyond belief. An access of madness is
punished as if it were an act of wilful insubordina-
tion. They are kicked and cuffed without mercy, and,
when they persist in making a noise, thrown vio-
lently down on the floor of their cells and compelled
to lie there. This within the hearing of the other
prisoners, who are rendered still more wretched by
the spectacle of so much suffering and cruelty, and
the consciousness of their inability either to prevent
the one or avenge the other.

The insane receive no indulgence in matters of discipline. They are compelled to observe the same
rules as the sane, and undergo the same penalties
for neglect or disobedience. Bogoluboff, condemned,
for the part he took in the demonstration in Kazan
Place, to fifteen years' hard labour (the same who was
flogged by order of General Trepoff, and avenged by
the pistol of Vera Zassoulitch), had a fixed idea that

everybody about him was in a conspiracy to take his life. Yet he was compelled to be shaved just as the others were. When the barber came to perform his offices the poor wretch screamed with terror and resisted with the fury of despair. But it was of no use. The warders throttled and pinioned him, and he was shaved whether he would or no.

When in April, 1879, a general, deputed by the new governor of the province, made an official visit to the Central Prison, asked the prisoners the stereotyped question, "Have you anything to say to me —any request to make?" one of the Circassians, Prince Zizianoff, made this answer:

"Yes, General. I ask a favour which you may easily grant. I ask to be condemned to death. Living here—which means slowly dying—is more than I can bear. I beseech you to put me out of my misery. I beg of you to let me die."

This answer, which I translate literally, is a full summing up, a complete picture. Comment were useless.

So we leave the Central Prison, with its horrors and sufferings, its martyred prisoners and tyrant gaolers; and I invite the reader to accompany me to another region and other scenes. But I warn him to brace up his nerves, for the tale I am about to unfold is still more terrible than that to which he has just listened.

CHAPTER XIX.

On the banks of the Neva, over against the Imperial Palace, stands the Russian Bastille—the Fortress of Peter and Paul. An immense building, wide and flat, surmounted by a meagre, tapering, attenuated spire like the end of a gigantic syringe. As it is situate between the two quarters of the town, the public may, during the day, pass through the fortress, entering by a narrow defile of sombre and tortuous vaults, occupied by sentinels, with the images of saints, holding burning tapers, in the niches. But at sunset all is closed, and when night broods over the capital, and thousands of lights illumine the quays of the swift-flowing Neva, the fortress alone remains in darkness, like a huge black maw ever open to swallow up all that is noblest and best in the unhappy city and country which it curses with its presence. No living sound comes to break the

grim silence that hangs over this place of desolation.
And yet the lugubrious edifice has a voice that
vibrates far beyond this vast tomb of unknown
martyrs, buried by night in the ditches, far beyond the *oubliettes,* where lie those whose turn is to
come next. Every quarter of an hour the prison
clock repeats a tedious irritating air, always the
same—a psalm in praise of the Tzar.

Here, indeed, is the altar of despotism. From its
very foundation the Fortress of Peter and Paul has
been the principal political prison of the empire.
But there is a wide difference in the character and
position of the unfortunates who have been its involuntary tenants. In past centuries the chief
sojourners were court-conspirators on their way to
Siberia or the scaffold. One of the first was the unhappy Prince Alexis, son of Peter the Great; pre-
sumptive heir to the crown. They still show you the
cell where the poor wretch, after being put to the
torture, was strangled by his father's order. Then
came generals, senators, princes, and princesses ;
among others the celebrated Tarakanova, drowned
during the floods that inundated the subterranean
cells of the fortress. Since the definitive establishment of the present dynasty, at the end of the last
century, palace conspiracies and *coups d'état* have
ceased. The fortress remained empty till 1825, when

it received the *élite* of the Russian nobility and
army—the Decembrists, who had not sought to overthrow one man in order to put themselves in his
place, but to destroy the principle of autocracy itself.

Two generations pass—and again the picture is
changed. Discontent with the present *régime* has
deepened and spread among all classes. It is no
longer the army, but the flower of the Russian
people that is rising against despotism ; it is no
longer an isolated attack, but an implacable war,
without truce or intermission, between the Russian
nation and its Government. The fortress is crowded
with prisoners. During the last twenty years hundreds have passed through it, and are being followed
by more hundreds, without pause or let.

But until lately the fortress was a " preventive "
rather than a penitentiary prison ; those accused of
political crimes were kept here pending their trial,
after which they were usually sent to the bagnios of
Siberia. There has, nevertheless, been here at all
times a certain number of prisoners—and these the
most wretched and rigorously guarded—sent without
any formality of trial, simply on a personal order of
the Tzar, and kept in prison for years together, often
for life.

In the ravelin of Alexis there is, or was in 1883, a
mysterious prisoner, a woman dying of consumption,

of whom no one—neither gaolers nor political prisoners —knows the crime or even the name, and who in the prison registers is merely designated by the number of the cell she occupies.

In the not very remote past, before the bureaucracy had succeeded in destroying all individuality, even in the despotism itself, the number of prisoners in the last-named category was much greater than at present. The fortress, with its flinty dungeons, was always ready to swallow up all who might make themselves disagreeable to the master of the hour. For Russia, being a Christian country, there were scruples about adopting the rough Oriental expedient of sewing up objectionable persons in canvas bags and casting them into the sea. In the course of ages, and under a despotic *régime,* this use of Peter and Paul naturally became more frequent and regular, and its advantages better understood. The point never lost sight of was the necessity of seeing that those who were buried alive in its gloomy recesses, depositaries of dark and shameful secrets, both of the masters and their acolytes, should never have the chance of revealing them to living soul. Hence the practice of covering a man's identity with a number as with an iron mask, and concealing his name, origin, and antecedents, a practice, however, of ancient date. Those of our historians who are allowed to search the archives of the secret police often find orders for the incarceration and detention of persons whose names the director of the fortress is forbidden, at his peril, to demand, or to ask any questions concerning them. The warders who took one of these men his food went in fear, and hastened away as quickly as possible, lest a chance word spoken by the mysterious prisoner might bring him into the torture chamber of the suspicious secret chancellery.

No wonder that there has always been an abundance of strange stories and fantastic rumours about this awesome prison-house, and that the popular imagination, taking hold of them, has added legend to legend. One arose out of the revolt of the Decembrists, which, as the people believed, was favoured by the Tzar's eldest brother, the Grand Duke Constantine, heir-presumptive to the throne, and to whom the country swore allegiance before it became known that he had secretly abdicated in favour of Nicolas. The rising created the myth of the Grand Duke being shut up in the fortress, a grey, decrepit old man, with a long white beard reaching to his knees, whose one thought and desire was to redeem the peasants from slavery. Years after the real Constantine, who led a savage and brutal life, had joined his ancestors, the legend still lived in the popular imagination.

But the spirit of the age and the crowds who now fill the fortress are not propitious for the creation of phantoms, and myth and legend are evolved no more. The reality is enough. On the other hand, the habits and ideas formed during a century and a half have been transmitted from one generation of gaolers to another, all animated by the same spirit. In the officers of the fortress the Government possesses an incomparable staff of warders, as well fitted for their duties as the mutes of some Grand Signior's seraglio.

The fortress differs from most other gaols, in that everything about it—*personnel*, organization, and description—are strictly military. There are no civil and salaried warders as in the Preventitive and Central Prisons. All the duties are performed by soldiers and gendarmes, over whose heads is ever hanging the Damocles sword of the military code. The charge over prisoners, whom it is desired to keep strictly in solitary confinement, is confided to gaolers carefully selected from among their fellows by a system of supervision and mutual espionage. This is the more easily done as the fortress, like all similar constructions built on the design of Vauban, is divided into bastions, curtains, and ravelins, every one of which forms a totally distinct prison, with its own director and staff of warders, who are never changed, live quite by them-

VOL. I.   15

selves, and seldom come in contact with any officers of the prison not belonging to their own section.

The fortress, moreover, differs from other prisons in the details of its organization, the strictness of its supervision, and the severity of its discipline. Thus, whilst in most other gaols it is considered sufficient to prevent prisoners from communicating with each other, in the fortress they are not allowed to communicate even with the warders. The latter are forbidden to answer any question put to them by a prisoner, however trivial or innocent it may be. A friendly greeting, an observation on the weather, an inquiry about the hour, it is all the same—no answer. In silence they come to your wicket, in silence they hand in your bread, in silence they depart. At the time fixed for the daily walk they open in silence your cell door, and in silence lead you to the yard set apart for exercise. Silently they watch you take your "solitary constitutional," and when it is finished re-conduct you to your cell without having once opened their mouths. "They," because there are always two, the warders of the fortress being absolutely forbidden to enter a prisoner's cell, or even go near a prisoner, under any pretext whatever, except in pairs. The advantages of this regulation are self-evident; it acts as a check, as well on prisoners as on officers, and facilitates that system of mutual espionage among the members of its staff which is one of the most characteristic features of the Russian Bastille.

The vast size of the building and its peculiar construction enable the Government to do here what they have vainly attempted to do elsewhere —completely isolate the prisoners among themselves. In the House of Preventitive Detention the numerous iron pipes which run through every part of the building, permit the inmates, even when separated by a considerable interval, to exchange messages; while in the Central Prison the cells are so small and the walls so thin that it is impossible to prevent the prisoners from talking by raps and, when they accidentally meet, by spoken words. In the fortress it is altogether different. The walls of the casements, laid in concrete and built of brick, are of a thickness that renders audible rappings, and consequently communications, almost impossible. To make them altogether so it was at one time (in 1877-8) proposed to deaden the sounds by coating the walls with felt. But as the adoption of this expedient, besides being expensive, would have made the cells drier and warmer, and the prisoners more comfortable, it was renounced in favour of a plan which possessed neither of these drawbacks. Prisoners were put only in every alternate cell, the intervening cells being either left empty or occupied by gendarmes. This entailed some reduction in the number of their inmates; but the fortress is very large, and those who remained were better cloistered. As to prisoners whom it was desired to isolate absolutely special arrangements were made.

To give an idea how complete these arrangements are, how well the great State prison of the Tzar keeps its secrets, a single example will suffice. Netchaef, surrendered by Switzerland, and condemned as an ordinary law-breaker to twenty years at the hulks, instead of being sent thither, was sent to the fortress (1872), and so closely guarded and immured that for seven years none of his friends knew what had become of him; albeit during this period incessant inquiries were made by many who were interested in his fate, and hundreds of prisoners entered and left the fortress. Not until 1880 was the place of his reclusion discovered, through the intermediary of Shiraeff, a prisoner in the Alexis ravelin, who had secret relations with the outer world, and to whom Netchaef, who was also confined in the ravelin, had contrived to send a message by a friendly gaoler.

As may be supposed, the treatment of prisoners incarcerated in this Russian Bastille does not err on the side of leniency, nor did it become more humane during the last Terrorist period, which was precisely the time when its dark and lonesome cells received the greatest number of inmates. If in the Central Prison, thousands of miles from the scene of action, the propagandists were made to "pay dearly" for every Terrorist attempt, it may be taken for granted that those of them who were in bonds at St. Petersburg would not fare better at the hands of their enemies. As a matter of fact, they fared worse. They were the victims of every sort of insult and violence, the commission of which was regarded as proof of loyalty and official zeal, and their complaints —if they had dared to make any—would either have passed unheeded or been answered by an insulting laugh or a cynical sneer.

But there is always a lowest depth, and in the place of torment which the fortress in these later days has become, a dungeon-house—human slaughter-house, rather—has recently been contrived, the horrors of which surpass anything that Englishmen can imagine. This is the Troubetzkoi ravelin. It is not a preventitive prison where suspected people await judgment, but a penitential gaol where convicts condemned for life or very long terms are confined and punished—a sort of bagnio to which are consigned those for whom the bagnios of Siberia or the cells of the Central Prisons are not considered sufficiently severe. Hither, too, are sent the Terrorists, whom their great numbers hindered from being hanged. Converted to its present purpose towards the end of 1881, or about the beginning of 1882, this dungeon within a dungeon has from the first been placed under the most rigorous supervision, and strict precautions taken to prevent knowledge of what goes on in its dark interior from coming to light. Three letters from prisoners have nevertheless passed the barriers, and reached the hands for which they were destined. They tell a tale which has thrilled educated Russia with pity and indignation, and reveal horrors to match which in Western Europe we must go back centuries. Two of these letters were written in haste and very briefly; they are little more than heartrending cries of suffering and despair. The third and most important is long and full of detail. It was printed forthwith in the clandestine press of the *Narodnaia Volia* under the title of, "Torture at the Bagnio of St. Petersburg in 1883." Though he had contrived to get a pen and some paper, the writer was compelled to write with his own blood, which (in the absence of a knife) he obtained by biting his flesh. This is a common device in Russian prisons, and we often receive letters written not alone metaphorically, but literally, with their author's blood. It was this blood-written letter that so deeply moved the lettered public of St. Petersburg, and from which some extracts appeared in the columns of the *Times* in June, 1884. To this very blood-written letter (which I have had in my hands), supplemented by information given by the two other letters, I am indebted for the following particulars.

Prisoners are generally transferred to the Troubetzkoi ravelin a few weeks after their conviction. You are told one fine morning, at a time perhaps when when you are in daily expectation of being sent to Siberia, that you must change your cell. You are ordered to don a regular convict suit, the principal garment of which is a grey coat, ornamented with a yellow ace. Preceded by one gendarme and followed by another, you are then led through a maze of passages, corridors and vaults, until a door, which seems to open into the wall, is reached. Here your conductors stop, the door is opened, and you are told to enter. For a minute or two you can see nothing, so deep is the gloom. The coldness of the place chills you to the bone; and there is a damp mouldy smell like that of a charnel house or an ill-ventilated cellar. The only light comes from a little dormer window, looking towards the counterscarp of the bastion. The panes are dark grey, being overlaid with a thick covering of dust, which seems to have lain there for ages. When your eyes have become accustomed to the obscurity, you perceive that you are the tenant of a cell a few paces wide and long. In one corner is a

bed of straw, with a woollen counterpane—as thin as
paper—nothing else. At the foot of the bed stands a
high wooden pail with a cover. This is the *parashka*,
which later on will poison you with foul stenches.
For the prisoners of the Troubetzkoi bastion are not
allowed to leave their cells for any purpose whatever,
either night or day (except for the regulation exercise), and the *parashka* is often left unemptied for
days together. You are thus obliged to live, sleep,
eat and drink in an atmosphere reeking with corruption and fatal to health. In your other cell you had
a few requisites, generally considered indispensable
for all men above the level of savages, such as a
comb, a hair brush, and a piece of soap. You were
also allowed to have a few books, and a little tea and
sugar, obtained, of course, at your own expense.
Here you are denied even these poor luxuries, for by
the rules of the Troubetzkoi ravelin prisoners are forbidden the possession of any object whatever not
given to them by the administration, and as the administration gives neither tea nor sugar, neither brush
nor comb nor soap, you cannot have them. Worse
still is the deprivation of books. In no part of the
fortress may books be brought from without. Ordinary prisoners must content themselves during all
the years of their solitary confinement with such as
are contained in the prison library, a few hundred

volumes, consisting, for the most part, of magazines dating from the first quarter of the century. But to the doomed captive of the Troubetzkoi—doomed to a fate worse than death—are interdicted books of every sort. "They may not read even the Bible," says the letter. No occupation, either mental or manual, beguiles the wretched monotony of their lives. The least distraction, the most trifling amusement, is as strictly forbidden to them as if it were an attempt to rob their gaolers, who exact from their victims all the suffering which it is in the power of the latter to give. A prisoner, named Zoubkovski, having made some cubes of bread crumbs .wherewith to construct geometric figures, they were taken from him by the gendarmes, on the ground that a prison was not a place of amusement. According to the regulations, the prisoners of the Troubetzkoi should have precisely the same amount of walking exercise as any other prisoners of the fortress. In point of fact, however, they are taken out only every forty-eight hours, to breathe the fresh air for ten minutes—never longer—and it sometimes happens to them to be left three and four consecutive days in the fetid atmosphere without break, as would appear, for no other cause but the neglect of the warders.

The rations allowed by the Government are quite insufficient, and of poor quality; but, bad as they are, the prisoners do not get them, for the purveyors (who are also managers of the prison), in order to economize on the official allowance, buy the worst and cheapest food they can lay their hands on—of course stealing the difference.* The flour is always bad, the meat seldom fresh. In order to make the bread weigh heavier, it is so insufficiently baked, that even the crust is hardly eatable, and when the inside of a loaf is thrown against the wall, it sticks there like mortar. Here is the daily *menu* of a Troubetzkoi prisoner : Three pounds of black bread, quality as described; in the morning, a jug of yellowish water, supposed to be tea ; at 11 o'clock, half a jug of kvas ; † at noon, a plate of soup made of bread crusts and sour cabbages, porridge of damaged Indian meal, and—except a few bits of meat, never exceeding three-quarters of an ounce, mixed with the soup— nothing more ; in the evening, another plate of sour soup, much diluted with water and without the least trace of meat.

---

* In past times things were managed differently. The fortress, being then an aristocratic prison, the prisoners had dinners of three courses, with white bread and even wine, and the linen was clean and fine. This went on, by routine, after the aristocratic prisoners were succeeded by the first Nihilists. But towards the latter end of the last Tzar's reign the fortress was democratised, and placed on the same footing as all the other prisons.

† The national drink : a sort of sour cider, or rather, acidulated water.

The prison is no better warmed than the prisoners are fed, a terrible hardship at sixty degrees of north latitude in the winter time. The cells are always cold, the walls always damp. When the inspector makes his round he never takes off his fur pelisse. The prisoners, who have no furs, shiver even in their beds, and all through the long winter their hands and feet feel like lumps of ice. Even in summer the prisoners are not in much better plight, for during the warmer months St. Petersburg, built on a marsh, is more unhealthy than at any other time. The unfavourable hygienic conditions of the fortress, the dampness of the cells, the lack of sunlight, the continual presence of the malodorous *parashka*, the bad and scanty food (worse in summer than in winter), aggravate the misery of the prisoners and fatally injure their health. The mortality among them is frightful. The most robust are unable to resist the unwholesome influence to which they are exposed; they wither like flowers deprived of water and air. While their bodies lose flesh, their faces become swollen and blotched, and the extremities, especially the hands, are in a continual nervous tremble. It might be supposed that the deprivation of books and the gloom of their cells would tend to preserve their eyesight. But it is the very reverse. Their eyes become inflamed, the lids swell and are opened only with great difficulty. But the maladies most fatal and frequent —which cause the greatest mortality and entail the most cruel suffering — are dysentery and scurvy, both caused solely by the insufficient and unsuitable dietary of the prison. Yet the sick are treated in exactly the same way as the whole; get the same food—same sodden black bread, same sham tea, even the same sour soup, which in their condition is nothing less than poison. No wonder that under such a regimen and without proper care —without any care at all — patients suffering from these disorders die quickly. They lose the use of their legs, they cannot reach the *parashka*, the warders refuse to change the straw of their wretched beds, and they are left to perish and rot in their own corruption. But these are horrors that defy description—that only the pen of a Dante could adequately portray.

" Oh, if you could see our sick! " exclaims· the writer of the blood-written letter. "A year ago they were young, healthy, and robust. Now they are bowed and decrepit old men, hardly able to walk. Several of them cannot rise from their beds. Covered with vermin, and eaten up with scurvy, they emit an odour like that of a corpse."

" But is there no doctor ? " it may be asked; and " What is he doing all this time ? " Yes, there is a doctor; there are even two doctors. One, however, is past fourscore and past work. He comes to the fortress only occasionally. The other is young, and probably kind enough in intention, but not very resolute in character, and standing in great awe of the officers of the gaol. When he visits his patients he is invariably accompanied by a brace of gendarmes, lest he should surreptitiously convey letters to prisoners. He enters the cell with a troubled countenance, as if he were afraid of something; never goes further than the threshold, much less approaches the sick man's bed or makes any examination of him, feels his pulse or looks at his tongue. After asking a few questions he delivers his verdict, which is almost always couched in the same words: "For your illness there is no cure."

And what better can the poor man do—what else say? According to the regulations enforced in the Troubetzkoi no indulgence can be shown to the sick: they must have the same food as the others — or none; no extra service is offered, no nurses are allowed them. The water is, moreover, so bad that, if other conditions were favourable, this cause alone would almost render recovery hopeless.

"No mercy is shown even to the mad," says another of the letters, "and you may imagine how many such there are in our Golgotha. They are not

sent to any asylum, but shut up in their cells and
kept in order with whip and scourge.   Often you
hear down below you, or at some little distance, the
sound of heart-rending shrieks, cries, and groans.
It is some wretched lunatic, who is being flogged into
obedience."

The following extracts from the Troubetzkoi regulations fully confirm the prisoners' statements concerning the stringency of the discipline imposed upon
them and the barbarous treatment to which they
are exposed—

"Prisoners of the Troubetzkoi, as bagnio slaves, are placed under
the administration of the fortress. For slight offences the administration may order a prisoner to be put from one to six days in a penal
cell, on a diet of bread and water, or sentence him to corporal punishment, the said corporal punishment to consist of not more than 20
stripes of the knout, or 100 strokes with a whip. In case of serious
offences (attempted escape, or resistance to authority) the culprit is
relegated to the military tribunal, which may order the infliction
of 100 stripes of the knout, 100 strokes with a whip, and as many as
8000 blows with a stick."

Thus the political prisoners of the Troubetzkoi
ravelin, mostly men of culture and refinement, and
belonging to the higher grades of society, have ever
before them the possibility of being compelled to
undergo corporal punishment in its cruellest and
most degrading form.   "We have every reason to
believe," says one of the letters in question, "that the
threat (of a flogging) is no empty one.   Zlatopolsky

was flogged for carrying on a secret correspondence with the help of a gendarme."

" Is it possible to remain quiet," exclaims the writer of another letter, " while the menace of such an outrage hangs continually over your head; while every cry you hear makes you feel as if one of your friends was being knouted before your eyes ! "

Nor is this the worst. There are women in the Troubetzkoi.

"What is most frightful," continues the writer, "is the position of the women, condemned like ourselves. Like us, they are at the mercy of their gaoler's caprices. No consideration is shown their sex. Their beds, like ours, are searched every day by men. The linen which they have just taken off is examined, at all times, by gendarmes. Nor is this all. Gendarmes may enter their cells day or night, just as they please. It is true that a rule forbids one gendarme to enter the prisoners' cells save in the company of another gendarme. But who cares for the infraction of such a rule? The relations between the various gaolers being of the most cordial nature, nothing is easier for them than to come to an understanding among themselves. Cases of rape are therefore very possible. At any rate attempts of this sort are common enough. Quite recently a young girl (one of the accused in the Odessa trial, L. Terentieva) has died most mysteriously. It is reported that she was poisoned by some venomous substance, administered by mistake in her medicine. There was, however, a rumour that this unhappy young girl, after being violated, was poisoned to prevent her from exposing the crime. It is, at any rate, certain that her death was for a long time kept secret from the superior police and gendarmery, that no inquiry has been instituted, and that the doctors have retained their posts."

Such are the horrors of prison life in the Troubetzkoi ravelin !

Shut out from all, surrounded by cruel and insolent

gaolers, who never speak except, perchance, to answer a harmless question with a gross insult, the captives become at last utterly cowed and moodily silent, living in their lonesome dens without a thought, without a future, and without a hope. If a prisoner can hold no secret communication with his friends, he loses count of the days, then of the weeks, then of the months. If he be sick and unable to leave his cell for exercise, he even ceases to observe the seasons; for whatever may be the weather outside, his dreary abode is always cold, gloomy, and damp, and his existence becomes a chaos which can end only in madness or death.

And even yet all the terrors of the Troubetzkoi are not told.

Under the first floor, and below the level of the Neva, are other cells far worse than those I have described—real underground vaults, dark at noonday and infested with loathsome vermin. They are the condemned cells, provided by the Government for those it most hates, and whom it has doomed to die either in lonesome darkness, or on the scaffold and in the light of day. Let us see what the letter has to say about this pandemonium :—

"The small windows are on a level with the river which overflows them when the Neva rises. The thick iron bars of the grating, covered with dirt, shut out most of the little light that else might filter through these holes. If the rays of the sun never enter the cells of the upper floor, it may easily be imagined what darkness reigns below. The walls are mouldering, and dirty water continually drops from them. But most terrible are the rats. In the brick floors *large holes have been left open for the rats to pass through.* I express myself thus intentionally. Nothing would be easier than to block up these holes, and yet the reiterated demands of the prisoners have always been passed by unnoticed, so that the rats enter by scores, try to climb upon the beds and to bite the prisoners. It is in these hideous dungeons that the condemned to death spend their last hours. Kviatkovsky, Presniakoff, Soukanoff, passed their last nights here. At the present moment, among others, there is a woman, with a little child at her breast. This is Jakimova. Night and day she watches over her babe lest he should be devoured by the rats."

"But," I hear my readers exclaim, "can these things be? Is it possible that at the end of the nineteenth century, in a great capital which wears at least the outward semblance of civilization, deeds so monstrous and cruel can be perpetrated? These letters written by men languishing in a wearisome captivity, and dwelling continually on their sufferings, are they not unconscious exaggerations?"

I should be glad to think so. I have no desire to paint with too dark a brush. But, as there is abundance of direct and indirect evidence to show, the statements set down by these necessarily nameless prisoners with their own blood are unfortunately only too true.*

---

* It is well to remember that the extracts from the letter in question, published in the *Times*, went the round of the European Press, and that the Russian Government has never ventured either to dispute their genuineness or disprove their statements.

From October 25 to 30, 1880, there were tried at
St. Petersburg sixteen Terrorists, six of whom were
condemned to death and eight to hard labour for
different terms. Two of the former were executed and
four reprieved. When the procurator, Aksharamoff,
informed the four that the Emperor had been pleased
to commute their sentences to penal servitude for
life, his news was received with such unmistakable
manifestations of disappointment and displeasure,
that he retired in confusion, observing that he could
not, unfortunately, change the decrees of the sovereign. And the prophetic souls of the prisoners did
not deceive them. The greater part of these young
and vigorous men (including those who were sentenced to hard labour) either died or went mad
before they had been in the fortress two years.
Isaieff, Okladsky, Zuekerman, and Martynovsky are
mad, Schiraeff is dead, Tichenoff is dying.

From facts like these only one inference is possible.

What must be the system that produces so dire
results ! Even if the blood-written letters were not
there to tell us, we could have no doubt.

Another fact. On July 26, 1883, there arrived at
Moscow a number of political convicts of both sexes
deported to Siberia, who had been imprisoned in the
Fortress of St. Peter and St. Paul ; and the following
is the description given by an eye-witness—eminently

trustworthy—of the condition to which these prisoners, whose crimes, it should be borne in mind, despite their severe sentences, were not deemed serious, had been brought by one years' detention in the cells of the Troubetzkoi ravelin :—

"The arrival of the St. Petersburg train caused great commotion amongst the officials and others who were in the station. Most of the prisoners could not alight without help, some even were unable to move. The guard wanted to transfer them straightway to our train, so as to conceal. their condition from the public. But this was quite impossible. Six of the prisoners fainted outright. The others could hardly stand. On this the chief of the escort ordered litters to be brought. But as the litters could not be got into the carriages, the unconscious prisoners had to be lifted out, like corpses, and carried on men's shoulders.

"The first man brought out was Ignat Voloshenko (sentenced first to ten years' hard labour in the Osinski trial, secondly, to fifteen years' hard labour for attempting to escape from Irkoutsk, then transferred to Kara, and afterwards to the fortress, where he had been kept one year). It is difficult to describe the horrible appearance and condition of this man. Eaten up with scurvy, he was more like a putrefying corpse than a living being. Torn every moment by convulsion—dying. . . . But it is useless. I am utterly unable to speak of him more.

"After Voloshenko was lifted out Alexander Pribylev (condemned in the trial of June 17, 1882, to fifteen years' penal servitude). He had no scurvy, but long abstention from food and complete derangement of the nervous system had so reduced his strength that he could not stand and frequently fainted.

"Next came Fomin (a former military officer sentenced for life).* He looked like a corpse, and for nearly two hours several doctors tried in vain to bring him round. It was not until evening that he was sufficiently restored to resume his journey.

"Fomin's successor was Paul Orlov (first sentenced to ten years at the hulks, subsequently to twenty-one years for trying to escape, and put with Voloshenko in the fortress, where he had been kept a year). Only twenty-seven years of age and once remarkable for his stature and strength, he was now hardly recognizable. He was bent like an old man, and one of his feet was so crippled that he could scarcely walk. He had scurvy in its most terrible shape, blood was continually oozing from his gums and flowing from his mouth.

---

* In 1882 he was at Geneva, a strong man, the very picture of health.—S. S.

"The fifth was a woman, Tatiana Lebedeva,* whose sentence of death (February 15, 1882) had been commuted to penal servitude for life. But imprisonment for Tatiana, whether long or short, had lost its terrors. Her days were numbered, and the greatest boon her enemies could bestow on her would be speedy death. Besides being in the last stage of consumption and torn with a terrible cough, she was so eaten up with scurvy that her teeth were nearly all gone, and the flesh had fallen away, leaving her jawbones quite bare. Her aspect was that of a skeleton, partly covered with parchment-like skin, the only sign of life being her still bright black eyes.

"After Lebedeva came Yakimova, holding in her arms an eighteen months' old babe born in the Troubetzkoi ravelin. The most hard-hearted could not look at that poor child unmoved. It seemed as if every moment would be its last. As for Yakimova, she did not appear to have suffered very much, either morally or physically, and, notwithstanding the penal servitude for life which was before her, bore herself with composure and firmness."

In view of facts like these it is impossible to delude

---

* Some twenty-eight years of age. She was of delicate constitution, but before being arrested, in 1881, in excellent health.

ourselves with the hope that the picture of their lives, drawn by the prisoners of the fortress in the letters I have cited, are in the least overdrawn, even unconsciously.

*   *   *   *   *

If the *régime* of preventitive detention and interrogation are virtually a reproduction of the judicial tortures of the Middle Ages, that of penitential imprisonment is an altogether new and original system, begotten of the baseness and cruelty of the Russian Government. Too craven to execute men and women publicly and by the dozen, it kills by inches—yet none the less surely—those of whom, either out of policy or revenge, it desires to rid itself. Torture daily repeated is the means, death not too long delayed the end. Because, if solitary confinement at Novo-Belgorod be, as the prisoner Zizianoff avers, and there is abundant evidence to prove, *slow* death, the same cannot certainly be said of incarceration in the black holes of the Troubetzkoi.

It is a portentous fact that the system of punitive or penitential imprisonment we have described has ceased to be an exception. It is becoming generalized throughout the empire, and the Russian Government are adopting it as part of a settled policy in their dealings with political offenders. Since 1878 no political convicts have been consigned to the Central

Prison, and the less seriously compromised alone are now transported to Siberia. Among the Terrorists none but those guilty of offences against State functionaries—and chiefly those of them who are women —are sent to the northern hulks; yet not until, like Tatiana Lebedeva and others, they have been brought to death's door by a term of penitential imprisonment. And still there are exceptions, for some, like Hessa Helfmann, Vera Figner, and Ludmila Volkenstein, were kept in the fortress. Hessa died there.

As for the Terrorists implicated in plots against the Emperor (of whom the majority naturally consists), they were consigned to the fortress one and all; yet how many of them are "finished," to use a Russian expression, or are in the course of being finished, we have no means of knowing, that being one of the secrets of the prison-house.

The Fortress of Peter and Paul is great. But there is a limit to everything—even to the capacity of a Russian Bastille—and to meet the ever-increasing demand for more accommodation, the Government of Alexander III. has deemed it desirable to provide another purgatory for its political prisoners—the fortress of Schlüsselburg. It is a second Troubetzkoi —no worse—and surely nothing can be worse! What still could the Government do more?—roast its prisoners alive, or do with them as the Roman emperors were sometimes wont to do with their enemies—throw them into holes swarming with vipers ?

But Schlüsselburg possesses in official eyes this priceless advantage—there is no chance of its horrors being exposed like those of the Troubetzkoi. Because Schlüsselburg is not in the middle of a great city, where there are thousands of sympathizers eager to communicate with the prisoners, and who, despite all the vigilance of the authorities, sometimes succeed in doing so. At Schlüsselburg nature herself acts as sentinel, for the new Castle of Despair is simply a huge block of granite covered with fortifications and surrounded by water. No news can be received, no secrets torn from that accursed prison. All who enter therein must abandon hope. From St. Peter and St. Paul volumes of clandestine letters have been received. The ravelins most jealously guarded—even the Alexis and the Troubetzkoi—have yielded their secrets to energy and perseverance. But from the prisoners in the Schlüsselburg—though they have been there for years—not a word, not a line ; only vague rumours. Yet it is thither that were sent the noble heroes of the latest trial—Lieutenant-Colonel Ashenbrenner, Captain Pokitonoff, and Lieutenant Tichonovitch. In Schlüsselburg, too, they have shut up fourteen propagandists, lately returned from Siberian hulks.

Here, also, let me add, there has been immured
for two years a man whose name I will not mention
—the friend of my boyhood, my fellow-worker in the
struggle.   On the eve of his removal to the Schlüsselburg he sent to us from the depths of the Troubetzkoi
ravelin this sublime farewell : "Fight on until the
victory is won.   For me henceforth there is but one
measure; the more they torment me in my prison
the better is it with the struggle."

By what ferocious language, by what fresh tortures
has he learnt the subsequent successes of his friends ?
Does he still continue to hear of them ?   Or is he,
perhaps, with so many others, where there is no more
to be suffered, no more to be learnt ?

CHAPTER XX.

SIBERIA.

SIBERIA ! The word sends a thrill of cold through our very bones, and when we think of the unfortunate exiles lost in icy wastes and condemned to life-long servitude in chains, our hearts are moved to pity and compassion. Yet, as we have seen, this word of horror is to some people suggestive of consolation and hope. To them it is a promised land, a place of security and rest. We know, too, that thither are sent men and women who, though reduced to the last extremity, their gaolers do not as yet want quite "to finish."

What, then, is this paradise of the lost, this enigmatical Siberian place of punishment, converted by a strange evolution into a Nihilist Kurort—a revolutionary sanatorium—as in a legend of the Plutonic realm its liquid fire is said to be turned into a cool and refreshing drink ?

Let us, taking the wings of imagination, cross the Uralian mountains, and flying far, far from the confines of Europe, descend in the region of Zabaikalia, beyond Lake Baikal, on the banks of the river Kara, see for ourselves what manner of life these Siberian transports lead.

But if we travel like ordinary mortals—and political convicts—we must, after leaving Irkoutsk by the Zabaikalia road, pass through Chita and Nertchinsk, celebrated for their "penitential mines," to Detensk. Here you take one of the Amour Navigation Company's steamers and journey by one of that river's affluents (the Shilke) to the little village of Oust-Kara, at the mouth of the river Kara, where there are several houses of detention for ordinary criminals and one for political convicts of the weaker sex. These prisons are detached buildings, standing on the river's bank, at intervals of from five to eight miles. All these prisons are under the general direction of a single chief; but the political prison, which consists of four buildings, has its own special organization and management. Twelve miles from Oust-Kara, and up stream, is the Lower Kara prison. Next comes that of Higher Kara; and, about the same distance further on, the Amour—that is to say, the prison on the river Amour.

A political prison is recognized by a characteristic

peculiarity. Other places of the sort—those destined for ordinary convicts—have outer walls or palisades on three sides only, the fourth being unenclosed with the front windows facing the road. Political prisons are arranged differently. Built in the middle of a court, they are surrounded on every side by walls so high that you can see only the roof. When the erection of these prisons was first proposed the architect designed it on the ordinary plan of similar structures in Siberia. But General Anutchin, at that time governor of Eastern Siberia, issued a special order that all gaols for political offenders were to be enclosed within lofty palisades in such a manner that the horizon of the inmates should be bounded by the wooden walls of their dreary abode. He thought this quite good enough for political prisoners.

The political prisons of Kara were organized at the same time as the Central Prison of Kharkoff. Their first tenants were Biberhal, Semenovsky, and others, of the first propagandists of 1872 and 1873. Next were sent thither the least compromised convicts of the trial of the 193 — Sinegoub, Tcharushin, and others.

From 1879 onwards prisoners arrived in crowds. In 1882 came the twenty-eight " centralists " (Kharkoff prisoners) liberated by Loris Melikoff from their worse than Babylonian servitude. In May of that year there were at Kara more than a hundred political prisoners, not counting women.

At the beginning of their confinement the Kara prisoners were treated precisely in the same way as other convicts are treated in Siberian lock-ups. The only exception was that, whereas ordinary criminals were allowed to walk freely in the yard during the day, the others were locked up in their rooms day as well as night—save, of course, when they were at work in the mines. These mines are the Emperor's personal property, and the prisoners are employed in removing the earth which overlays the auriferous sand. At Kara, as in Siberia generally, there exists a regulation very favourable to convicts under sentence of penal servitude. After having passed a third of their time in prison "under probation," they are allowed to join a "free gang," which gives them the privilege of living outside the prison walls, in towns and villages—always on condition that they remain there. At first, political prisoners enjoyed this privilege equally with other prisoners. Sinegoub, Tcharushin, Semenovsky, and others were provisionally set free in this way. It is a matter of everyday occurrence for ordinary convicts to profit by their comparative freedom to try to escape and join the great horde of vagabonds who throng Siberian roads. But it never occurred to the administration to curtail, on this account, the privileges of those who remained, or make them jointly and severally responsible for the conduct of their comrades. As touching the politicals, however, extreme precautions were adopted. The "free gangs" of "politicals" were told that at the first attempt on the part of any of their number to escape, the "free gang" system, so far as they were concerned, would be abolished. The administration, on the other hand, undertook that, so long as the political prisoners faithfully observed the regulations, this and all the other privileges should be respected. Though the prisoners, on their part, entered into no formal engagement to comply with these conditions, they did in effect faithfully observe them. Not once during the prevalence of the "free gang" system did there occur any disorder or any attempt to escape. Nevertheless the administration broke its word and withdrew the privileges.

This breach of faith was instigated by Loris Melikoff. At the very time the dictator was pretending to better the lot of political prisoners, posing as a man of exceptional benevolence and humanity, and, with a great flourish of trumpets, transferring people from the Central Prisons of Kharkoff and Mzensk to Kara, a peremptory order was issued withdrawing, as regarded political convicts, the "free gang" system, and remitting to gaol those who had been provisionally liberated. A strict interdict was laid on all correspondence between themselves and their kindred and friends.

The men who had only just been set at liberty, and were looking forward to permanent, if somewhat restricted freedom, had therefore to return to prison. This was very hard on the poor fellows, yet keenly as they felt the wrong they were compelled to resign themselves to their fate. The evening before they separated and went back to their cells they had a last supper. The meeting was sad, and their hearts, as may be supposed, were very heavy. For one member of the company it was indeed a last supper, and ended in a terrible tragedy. Semenovsky, maddened by despair, blew out his brains. In ill health, nervous, and with spirits broken by long confinement, the idea of returning to prison was intolerable to him. He preferred death. A man of high principle and wide culture, once an advocate in St. Petersburg, Semenovsky was sentenced on October 20, 1876, to a long term of penal servitude for simple propagandism. The administrator telegraphed the news of his tragic death to St. Petersburg. But it had no effect on the Government. Semenovsky was buried, and his companions were again put in prison.

Nor was this all. They were not only remitted

to confinement, but annoyed and teased past
bearing, and harassed with all sorts of petty vexations. New restrictions were placed on the visits
of the devoted wives who had followed their hus-
bands to this far-away and dreary land. It was
made more difficult for the sick to obtain admission
to the hospital. But the greatest grievance of all
was denying them the solace of labour. They were
forbidden to work in the mines. In the spring of
1882 this privilege, for as such they esteemed it, was
denied to them, a measure which greatly aggravated
the hardship of their lot. The hardest labour—
even the toil of the mines—was a lighter punishment than the sedentary and solitary monotony of
life within the four walls of their prison house. Mus-
cular exercise, besides doing them good physically,
made time pass less slowly and more pleasantly.
But all the efforts of the prisoners, and they were
many, to obtain the hard work to which they were
condemned proved abortive. It seemed as if the
administration was resolved to let them perish
slowly for want of air and exercise, like their friends
in the central prisons. If we consider that most of
these men were sentenced to very long terms—
twenty, thirty, and even thirty-five years—it is easy to
understand how ardently they must have longed for
freedom, how eager they were to escape. No wonder

that attempts to get away became thenceforth more frequent than before. How these attempts were dealt with by the authorities the following chapter will show.

CHAPTER XXI.

MUTUAL RESPONSIBILITY.

DURING the first May night of the year 1882 the sentinels of the political prison of Lower Kara noticed
a man attempting to escape by the workshop window
opening on the fields. Twice they fired on him, and
twice they missed aim. An alarm was sounded, the
prisoners were immediately mustered, and it was
found that eight of them, among whom was Myshkin, had escaped. When informed by telegraph of
what ·had come to pass, the Minister of the Interior was so angry that the governor of Zabaikalia,
General Iliashevitch himself, feared that he should
be dismissed for not exercising due vigilance, the
more so as about ten days before he had inspected
the prison together with the Senator Galkin-Vrasski,
and reported everything to be in perfect order.
Fearing for their places, the local administration
resolved to provoke a riot among the prisoners in

order to redeem their characters by its suppression, and to atone for the neglect that had caused the escape—which could then be explained by saying the rules were too lax, and that for prisoners so intractable ordinary supervision was not sufficiently severe.

On the 4th of May the prisoners were ordered, without further explanation, to shave their heads. They replied that, according to the rules they were allowed to wear their hair, and the rules being drawn up by the Minister of the Interior, he only, and not the director, had a right to change them.

On the 6th of the same month the political prisoners were officially informed that they would not be roughly dealt with, that all would go on as heretofore, and that they might make themselves easy. Five days passed in this way, and the prisoners were beginning to forget the incident. But they were reckoning without their host. The 11th of May was fixed for the riot and its suppression. About three in the morning six hundred Cossacks, under the command of General Iliashevitch himself, supported by Colonel Roudenko, surrounded the prison, occupied all the issues with platoons, and ordered the bulk of the force to rush upon the sleeping prisoners—of whom, it should be added, there were only eighty-four.

So soon as they were awake they were searched,

and all their belongings, down to the merest trifles—
books, clothes, combs, brushes—seized, and thrown
pell-mell into a corner. This done, the prisoners
were attired in convict dresses and taken into the
courtyard. Here twenty-seven "promoters" and
"instigators" of the "riot" were picked out, and led
under the escort of Cossacks to Upper Kara, a distance
of some ten miles. Encouraged by their officers,
the Cossacks grossly insulted and ill-used the prisoners during the journey, and when a few tried to
defend themselves Colonel Roudenko said, "Tie their
hands behind them, and if one of them says anything
impertinent give him a knock on the head with the
butt-end of your guns." Meantime the prison of Lower
Kara was being pillaged. Before the struggle began
Colonel Roudenko addressed the Cossacks thus:—
"If I order you to beat them, do so; if I order you
to fire, shoot them. When you have taken the prison
you shall have everything belonging to them." And
the Cossacks, having subdued the sleeping rioters, set
about pillaging their possessions. The officers, not
to be outdone by their men, appropriated some of the
best things—even carrying off tables, chairs, stools,
which had been made by the prisoners themselves,
and giving them to their friends.

After they had passed some time in the empty room,
with no other clothing than the grey regulation cloaks,

the deputy-director, Boutakov, appeared before the prisoners, one of whom asked :

" Is it possible that we are to remain in this state much longer ? "

"Yes, always," answered Boutakov. " You were formerly treated well, but now, after these escapes, we see that your conduct——"

Orloff observed that the administration itself had provoked the escapes, not the prisoners, and that in any case it was unjust to make those who remained suffer for those who had escaped.

This modest and polite answer put the deputy-director into such a rage that he ordered the Cossacks to seize Orloff, beat him, and drag him to the punishment cell. Some of his comrades wished to prevent this, but he besought them to offer no resistance. When he 'was outside the door, Colonel Boutakov rushed at him, began to strike him, and ordered the Cossacks to do the same. A little later—while the prisoners were dining—the director came in person, mustered them, and told them to " get up." Some did not obey with sufficient promptitude. " Make them get up with blows," ordered the director, and a fresh summary execution began. " This is the way to muster," said he, with great satisfaction, going out after the disturbance. In the next room a similar scene was being enacted, under the command of the captain of the guard. When he entered, the student Bobokhov was lying on the plank. The captain, turning to his Cossacks, ordered them to " drag him up by the hair," and by the hair he was dragged up.

Rodionoff, quite a young man, was also beaten by the director himself, who, when he was tired, handed the victim over to his Cossacks, telling them to "give him as much as he could carry." After this Rodionoff was put into the black hole for thirty days.

This took place at Lower Kara ; but the men who had been taken to the two other prisons came off no better, save that in one instance, at Upper Kara, the soldiers, to their honour, absolutely refused to beat them. Those at the Amour prison were more complaisant, thereby suggesting Gerasimoff's grim *bon mot,* " We are beaten twice a day, and fed once."

In the summer of 1882 the Lower Kara lock-up was rebuilt on a new plan. The large common rooms were divided into small cells, where five and six men were made to sleep together on the same bed, so tightly wedged that it was difficult to move, and impossible to turn. The prisoners who had been dispersed in the other gaols were brought back (except fourteen sent to Schlüsselburg as " promoters "), and everybody was put in irons. Three were chained (the chains being fastened with rivets) to wheelbarrows,

which they had, of course, to drag with them everywhere. Then, to render flight more difficult—or,
rather, recapture more easy—the left half of each
man's head was clean shaven, an operation which
was effected with some circumstance, the authorities
probably fearing that the indignity might be forcibly
resisted. The prisoners were called one by one into
a room, as they supposed, to be questioned touching
their knowledge of the escape. The victim was then
surrounded by soldiers, and asked if he would submit quietly; if not they threatened to tie his hands
and shave his head by force. Resistance in these
circumstances was, of course, not attempted.

All the work of the prison was done by the convicts
themselves; they cleaned their own rooms, washed
their own linen, and prepared their own meals. But
whatever they did they were under strict and continual supervision, being never left a moment to
themselves. Then, as if to fill the measure of their
misery to the full, a common malefactor, named
Ziploff, was brought amongst them. He had carried
letters between some of the political prisoners, an
offence which, as the administration chose to think,
qualified him for their company. Yet, so far from
approving of the change, Ziploff begged and prayed
to be allowed to go back to his old quarters. But the
administration had other views. One day he was

called into the office, charged with some trifling breach
of discipline of ancient date, and ordered to be flogged.
The punishment was duly inflicted under the personal
supervision of Commandant Kaltourin himself. What
this meant the others knew only too well. It was a
warning, an intimation made in the most forcible
way possible that the political prisoners were no
longer to enjoy immunity from corporal punishment;
and shortly afterwards it was rumoured that the
fugitives, all of whom had meanwhile been recaptured
(Myshkin at the very moment when he had got on
board an American ship at Vladivastock, bound for
San Francisco), would be publicly flogged. The cup
of their sufferings, already full to the brim, now ran
over. The prisoners resolved that, rather than submit to this new degradation, they would die; and,
notwithstanding the desire of a considerable minority
to adopt a more energetic form of protest, it was
decided that they should die of hunger.

Then began a long fast, a terrible ordeal for men
weakened with hardship and by confinement. All
went to bed, and were soon reduced by abstinence to
a state of utter prostration. In seven days they had
almost lost power of speech, and could not answer to
their names at roll call, a formality which takes place
three times a day. Then the directors, who had
hitherto cherished the hope that the prisoners, tor-

mented by the pangs of hunger, would give up the contest, saw that matters were come to a crisis. They entered the cells, regarded in silence the inanimate forms of the sufferers, and the gravity of their looks showed how much they were concerned. Next came Commandant Kaltourin, who, after asking what they wanted, had their demands put in writing, and promised to communicate immediately by telegraph with the governor of the province, Iliaschevitch. He assured them, moreover, on his own responsibility, that there was neither truth in the rumours they had heard, nor any intention to abolish the rules which proscribed the flogging of political prisoners. But as no confirmation of this statement was received from General Iliaschevitch the voluntary famine continued. But it could not go on much longer. The fasters were on the point of death. They suffered from convulsions, sleeplessness, and dysentery. A few, who from the first had objected to this form of resistance and taken no part in it, now adjured their companions to abandon the contest before it was too late. Their persuasions, together with something else that happened of great importance—the nature of which, however, our correspondent did not feel himself at liberty to mention—prevailed at last on the strikers to terminate their fast—on the thirteenth day after it had begun. This terrible struggle, which permanently injured the health of most of the prisoners who engaged in it, had no other result than a few concessions, and a not very definite assurance from the administration that their exemption from corporal punishment would be continued.

In this way did the administration avenge on the prisoners the abortive flight of a few of their companions. Nor was this the full extent of their punishment. Sixteen men, who at the time of what is known as "the revolt of the 11th of May" had finished their term, and were entitled, according to the regulations, to become free Siberian colonists, were kept in prison another year. Even political prisoners elsewhere (Kviatkovski, Zoubrilloff, and Frangeoli), who did not even know of the escapes, were dealt with in like manner. In 1883, however, they were released, those first set free being sent as colonists to the province of Baikal. But when Shoubin, the new commandant of the political prisons, reported to Governor Iliaschevitch that the Kara prisoners still manifested "a spirit of indocility," he ordered the colonists, and thirteen others whose terms had also expired— "by way of giving them a lesson"—to be exiled to a village in the far north, the region of the polar night, among the savage Yakutes, where life is, if possible, even harder than in the prisons. This is what they call in Russia "mutual responsibility."

Among the colonists was a young woman of the name of Maria Koutitonskaia, who, after the affair of May 11th, had been released from gaol and "interned" in a village of the province. That is to say, she was free to go about but not to go away. This girl-heroine resolved with her own hand to avenge the cruel outrages inflicted by the authorities on innocent and helpless prisoners. After obtaining a small revolver, she started secretly for Chita, where lived General Iliaschevitch, the Governor. Arrested as a fugitive, she was taken to Chita—exactly where she wanted to go. On her arrival thither she asked to see the Governor, saying that she wanted to explain to him personally why she had left Aksha. There being no reason why this request should not be complied with, she was taken straightway to the palace; and as General Iliaschevitch came out of his cabinet, Maria drew her revolver, and with the words, " This is the answer to the 11th of May," fired at him point blank. The ball struck the Governor in the abdomen, and he fell, badly wounded, to the ground. Maria was, of course, immediately arrested and put in prison. She was afterwards tried and condemned to death, but the Government deemed it expedient to commute this sentence to one of hard labour for life.

It is hardly necessary to say, however, that this incident had very little effect on the lot of the pri-

soners of Kara. The barbarities and cruelties we
have described went on without surcease.

Such is life in the political prisons of Siberia, the
promised land toward which revolutionists under
sentence of penal servitude turn longing eyes. And
it is certainly an improvement on the Fortress. On
the other hand, it is very little, if any, better than
detention in a Central Prison. If in this latter place
of punishment the torture inflicted on prisoners is
more sustained and systematic, in Siberian gaols they
are more exposed to the violence and brutality of
warders and guards; for long-continued immunity,
the absence of all control, and the evil traditions of
despotism, have transformed the gaolers of our hyper-
borean prisons into veritable tyrants. "For you I
am Chief, and Tzar, and God," is a stereotyped expression in the mouths of these Cerberuses, when
addressing a prisoner.

Time fails me to recount a hundredth part of the
known atrocities inflicted on the victims of despotism
in every part of Siberia, and on every possible pretext. And how much greater is the number of those
we do not, nor ever shall know!

But an instance of the sort of treatment which
women receive at the hands of the Siberian servants
of the Tzar is too relevant and characteristic to be
omitted.

The victim on this occasion was Olga Lioubato-vitch, one of the heroines of the trial of the fifty propagandists who, as the reader may possibly remember, won to so remarkable a degree the sympathy of the public. On August 30, 1883, as Olga (who once escaped from Siberia, reached Geneva, then returned to Russia, only to fall a second time into the toils) was passing through Krasnoiarsk on her way to her destination in Eastern Siberia, she was called before the *ispravnik* (local chief of police) and ordered to change the dress she wore for the costume of a convict. But having been condemned to transportation by administrative order—not to hard labour—she had a right to wear her own clothes; and this she tried to make the *ispravnik* understand. At her first words, however, he became furious, and repeated that she must not only change her dress, but do it there and then in the bureau, before everybody. To this monstrous request Olga Lioubatovitch answered by a plump refusal. Then at a sign from the *ispravnik* his subordinates took hold of the prisoner and proceeded to undress her by force. A shameful struggle ensued. Several men set on this defenceless woman, beat her, pulled her hair, and tore off her clothes. So long as she kept her feet she defended herself as best she could, but the chief of the police by a violent kick felled her to the earth. What follows is best described in her own words :

"I fell into a kind of stupor. I remember confusedly how the heavy boot of the *ispravnik* struck my chest. Some one was pulling my hair, another was striking my face with his fists ; the rest were tearing off my clothes, and at last, naked, crucified on the floor, in the presence of a crowd of men, I felt all the shame and horror of a woman violated. Alarmed by their own deed, the cowards fled, and when I recovered consciousness I saw around me only my companions, pale as death, while Fanny Moreiness was writhing in hysterical convulsions."

But enough, enough ! The sufferings of the Nihilists are truly terrible, and, as being the noblest holocaust ever offered by patriots on the altar of a country's redemption, worthy of all sympathy and respect. Yet compared with the trials and sufferings of Russia at large they are only a drop—a bitter and burning drop, but not to be compared with the ocean of which they form so small a part.

Let us explore this ocean.

PART III.

ADMINISTRATIVE EXILE.

CHAPTER XXII.

INNOCENT THEREFORE PUNISHED.

THE judicial procedure, of which the complete cycle—
from arrest to punishment—we have already described, is far from including all the means employed
by the Russian Government in its struggle with
revolution.

Tribunals from their very nature must deal with
facts. However great may be their severity, however
willing they may be to conform to orders, impute
motives, and visit trifling misdeeds with draconian
punishments, they must, at least, have something to
go upon. In other words, they cannot convict a man
because he is innocent. If a person be found in
possession of a revolutionary proclamation, or if he
lends his room for revolutionary purposes, he may be
condemned to death; but if no overt act, no equivocal expression or compromising conduct whatsoever can be brought home to him, they are obliged to
pronounce a verdict of acquittal. This depends not

on the quality of the judges but on the nature of tribunals.

The ordinary methods of prosecution are therefore essentially circumscribed. They can be used only against offenders who have given some manifest sign of hostility to the existing system, or openly or covertly attacked the Government.

How then are those to be dealt with who have done none of these things, yet who, there is every reason to believe, will do them sooner or later?

Let us take an example. A man who has had secret relations with the revolutionary party and falls under suspicion is arrested, questioned, and badgered in the usual fashion, and kept in prison several months. But neither in his own admissions nor in any other way can a scintilla of evidence be found against him. In no single respect can he be considered a compromised person, and it is impossible, by any stretch of ingenuity, to include him in the indictment of those who are supposed to be his confederates and friends. So he is let out on bail, and subpœned as a simple witness. But by his conduct under examination and before the tribunal, by his unwillingness to testify against the accused and his eagerness to testify in their favour, he shows only too clearly that he is a sympathizer with them in spirit if not a confederate in fact.

Against another man, perhaps, the public prosecutor has succeeded in gathering some miserable
scraps of equivocal evidence, and so includes him in
the indictment. So equivocal is it, indeed, that the
tribunal, with all the will in the world to oblige the
procurator, has no alternative but either to acquit
the prisoner altogether or give him a nominal sentence. There is nevertheless good reason to believe
that this individual is just as *perverse* as those of his
friends who have allowed themselves to be taken in
the act, and been sentenced to penal servitude. Who
can say that this absence of proof is not the result of
pure accident? And even if he has done nothing so
far, what signifies that? It is only because he has
had no opportunity—that is all. Being a revolutionist in intention, he is sure to take action on the
first favourable occasion. It is merely a question of
time. Put him outside the court certainly, but only
that he may be forthwith re-arrested.

For how can the police let these men, whom they
have the chance of collaring, depart in peace? It
would be as bad as letting prisoners of war rejoin the
enemy. It cannot be done.

But let us leave judicial considerations to lawyers
and experts, and regard the question in another
aspect and from a general point of view. Let us
take the case of a man so free from reproach that he

can neither be arraigned as a prisoner nor called as a witness. But "from information it has received" (the reports of spies), the Government feels sure that he is a revolutionist. When this conviction is entertained about a man, absence of proof is held of no account. The police and procurators have a very high opinion of the integrity of their country's revolutionists. They firmly believe that these men always possess the courage of their opinions and act according to the dictates of their conscience. Want of evidence serves only to increase their suspicion. None who have had dealings with our procurators and gendarmes can fail to have heard, twenty times, the stereotyped phrase: "We know quite well there are no proofs against so and so — your husband, brother, sister, or friend — but that only makes them the more dangerous; it shows that they have arranged matters so cleverly that the police can find nothing out."

Once the wolf has been discovered under the lion's skin measures must be taken to disarm the enemy of order and society. If these words, "order" and "society," were understood in their accepted signification, an ordinary government might deem it expedient to wait a while and defer somewhat to considerations of general utility and public decency. But if "order" means its own skin, and "society" its own pocket, this becomes a psychological impossibility. A government ruling a nation as a conquered country, a government hemmed in by enemies on every side, with every thought concentrated on its own defence, and possessed of unlimited power to make that defence good—such a government as this was sure, sooner or later, to supplement the ordinary judicial procedure with another, a prompter, and a more subtle system, designed to redress its failures and correct its shortcomings—to do that which, in the nature of things, it was out of the question the former should do.

This system is known as the "administrative procedure." It involves a division of labour. The tribunal punishes, the administration prevents. The tribunal deals with acts, the administration with intentions. The tribunal searches people's houses and pockets, the administration looks into men's hearts and reads their thoughts.

When the administration has decided that a man has it in his mind to do them an ill turn, they place him under the supervision of the police.

In this, taken by itself, there is nothing extraordinary or extreme—at any rate, on the Continent, where it is quite in the common course of things to submit people to police surveillance. But between the practice of Germany and France and the practice of Russia there is this great difference: in the former countries only malefactors who have been tried and convicted are placed under supervision, whereas in Russia men are treated after this fashion who have been tried and acquitted, as also men who never have been tried or even accused. But wide as is this difference, it is not all. There is supervision and supervision. In its common acceptation the word means that the police will keep its eye upon you. How they do this is their affair and that of their spies. All that is required of you is to inform them of any change in your address. In Russia, however, it is very much otherwise. In Russia the marked man is required so to arrange matters that the supervisors shall have every facility for performing their task and be able to watch their man without giving themselves too much trouble. Suppose, for instance, that a man living at Odessa is ordered to be placed under supervision. The police, in that case, would probably declare it to be quite out of their power to supervise him effectually except at a place some thousand versts or more away. On this, our man would be promptly sent to the locality designated and forced to remain there until the police had done with him. Hence police supervision in Russia is but another name for administrative exile.

The right of putting people under surveillance,

which the Russian criminal code, like the codes of
France and Germany, reserves exclusively to the
courts of justice as a penitential measure, the administration exercises arbitrarily without the least
scruple. It orders into exile with equal indifference
persons who have been tried and acquitted, witnesses
who have testified truly, and citizens who, for some
inscrutable reasons, are simply suspected of latent
sedition. We therefore come to this — that the
liability of Russian subjects to be exiled is limited
only by the good pleasure of the gendarmery and the
police. Under the pretext that an exile's conduct
has not been satisfactory, moreover, the term of his
banishment may be indefinitely prolonged. Thus in
the affair of the Netchaeff Society (autumn, 1871), when
of eighty-seven prisoners thirty-three were convicted
and thirty-four acquitted, the latter were exiled with
hardly an exception, as also several witnesses whom the
procurator had not ventured to indict. Among the
exiled, as is well known, was Miss Vera Zassoulitch.
She passed several years in exile, and only recovered
her liberty by flight. Mr. Nikiforoff, a kinsman of
hers, and one of the witnesses on the trial, was also
exiled, and though fourteen years have elapsed is in
exile still.

Administrative exile played an important part even
during the first period of the revolutionary move-

ment. The thing was so common that when it was mentioned that these or those persons had been acquitted at this or that trial the first question asked was invariably, "And whither are they exiled?" This observation implied neither irony nor doubt—was so natural, indeed, that only the fact of their not being exiled would have called forth an expression of surprise. Sometimes the police play with their victim after the manner of a cat with a mouse. In 1878 Mr. Alexander Olkhin, a member of the St. Petersburg bar, being suspected of having secret relations with the revolutionary party—albeit there was not a shred of evidence against him—was exiled to Kholmogori in the government of Archangelsk. Two years later the police imagined they had found the desired proof, whereupon Mr. Olkhin was brought back to St. Petersburg and put on his trial. But the police had been in too great haste. The proofs were too flimsy even for the most pliable of tribunals; the prisoner was pronounced not guilty (the Mirsky trial, November, 1879). But this result had not the slightest effect on the police, they exiled Mr. Olkhin afresh, and his second condition was worse than his first.

To finish, I will cite a well-known name, that of Prince Alexis Krapotkin, brother to Prince Peter, a mathematician and astronomer who never concerned himself with politics. His fault was being akin to Peter and not showing sufficient respect for the gendarmes. In the autumn of 1876 the post-office having intercepted a letter which, as the police suspected, was destined for a political refuge whose acquaintance Alexis had made while travelling abroad, they searched his house. No confirmation of their suspicion was forthcoming, but the prince imprudently showed annoyance at this proceeding, treated the procurator and gendarmes with scant courtesy, and, to use an idiomatic Anglicism, "gave them a piece of his mind." Imprisonment produced no change in his demeanour, and in the end they sent him to Siberia. This came to pass nine years ago, and he is in Siberia still, ruined in health and bereft of his only son.

All the exiles of this period were banished by subterfuge. While nominally placed under police surveillance as a measure of precaution, they were sent to the confines of the empire as a matter of fact, and there detained. Thus was committed a double wrong. In the first instance, these people were punished without trial, in itself a gross illegality; in the second instance, they were not alone placed under surveillance without warrant, but this surveillance, equally without warrant, was converted by a piece of casuistry into a sentence of unlimited transportation. The code, it may be well to mention, recognizes no such thing as administrative exile. This, however, is a consideration which has little interest for Russians, and, save legists, few ever give it a thought.

In 1879, however, the reproach in question was removed, and for six years administrative exile has been a recognized bulwark of order and a regular Russian institution. On April the 2nd of the year in question, Solovieff attempted the Tzar's life. On the 6th—three days later—a new law was ordained whereby all Russia, habited and habitable, was divided in six regions, under the rule of six generals, each in his own region clothed with despotic powers. The local civil authorities were ordered to render these satraps the same obedience which they would render in a state of war to a general-in-chief. The six dictators, moreover, had the same powers as are wielded by a commander-in-chief in war time over all the inhabitants of their respective districts. These powers included (a) the right to exile by administrative order all persons whose continued stay in the district might be considered prejudicial (to public order) ; (b) to imprison at their discretion all persons, without distinction of rank or title, whenever they might find it advisable ; (c) to suppress, or provisionally suspend, any journal or review the tendencies of which might seem to them dangerous; and (*d*) generally take such measures as they might deem necessary for the maintenance of tranquillity and order in the regions over which they were placed.

This in Russia they call a law! Since April, 1879, therefore, administrative exile has become perfectly legal. In the same way, when the six satrapies were abolished, the country was placed in " a state of surety " (for surety read " siege "), and the exceptional powers entrusted to the generals were permanently conferred on the ordinary governors.

Since that time the system of administrative exile has received a great extension and become the favourite weapon of the Russian Government in its contest with the nation—so much so that *de facto* juridic procedure is relegated more and more to the background.

When Solovieff's attempt was followed by several others, the Government fell into a very paroxysm of panic and passion. It felt the ground shaking under its feet, it tried to spread terror everywhere, to strike hard, to tear up sedition by the roots. For this end exile was far more effective than the tribunals, with their forms, ceremonies, and delays; and on the least suspicion, real or feigned, the least sign or the flimsiest pretext, it was applied right and left. It became a pest, a devastation.

If, however, the reader were to ask me to define, more or less precisely, the signs and pretexts which the administration deem sufficient to justify the infliction of so severe a punishment as exile, I should find it difficult to give a satisfactory answer. Everything has its measure, even the susceptibility of the Russian police. As in chemistry there are substances whose presence is manifested by very energetic reactions, but the detection of which defies the most delicate scales, so it is with the police. Except in cases where personal antipathy or private vengeance is the motive (cases which are far from being exceptional), the police, before they tear a man from his family and his business, deprive him of his livelihood, and send him to the other extremity of the empire, must have *something* against him. What this something may be we can form an approximate idea from incidents that have actually occurred, cases in which it has been possible to obtain information as to the motives of the police in sending people into exile. In many instances it is impossible even to conjecture these motives, and I purposely confine myself to cases in which the victims have been of good social position, for to them the Government generally shows somewhat more consideration than to people of inferior rank.

We will begin with Mr. Petrounkevitch, land-

owner, member of the Zemstvo of Tchernigoff, and
president of the justices of peace of his district. In
May, 1879, this gentleman was arrested by order of
the Minister of the Interior, the ground assigned for
the proceeding being his dangerous opinions as manifested in an official report of the local Zemstvo,
drawn up by a commission, of which Mr. Petrounkevitch was the chairman, in answer to a ministerial
circular. He was taken in open day while busied
with his official duties ; and, without being allowed
to say a word to his family, hurried off under police
escort to Moscow, and sent thence to Varnavin, in
the government of Kestroma.

About the same time was arrested Dr. Bely, the
medical officer of the same Zemstvo. As his name
was not appended to the report in question, and he
took no part in the proceedings of the Zemstvo, the
" perversity " imputed to him could not be inferred
from his acts or his words—it had to be divined by
intuition, read in his heart. This duty was under-
taken by the parish priest of Ivangorod, a sort of
duty for which priests in general have a decided
predilection. He denounced Dr. Bely as " evil-
intentioned and a suspect " on the following grounds
(which I give textually): " That the doctor was
personally acquainted with Petrounkevitch, upon
whom he was in the habit of calling (in which,

seeing that they lived within a few miles of each other, there was surely nothing very extraordinary), and whose opinions, the perversity of which was well known, he shared." The priest alleged further that Dr. Bely showed a decided partiality for the company of peasants; that he seldom went into the town, where there was good society, preferring rather to remain in the village among his peasant neighbours; that he did not bestow sufficient care on the health of the local nobility, neglecting his patients of that class in order to give more time to his humbler patients; that in his hospital were two young ladies, one of whom wore the national folks' dress (this was Miss Bogolubova, who had been a sister of mercy in the army of the Balkans. She was arrested a few days after Dr. Bely, and exiled nobody knows whither). The facts set forth by the priest, leaving no doubt as to the doctor's perversity, Mr. Malakhoff, the *pristav* (subaltern officer of police), had him arrested on July 19th. He was first sent under escort to Vychny-Volotchek, and then exiled to Eastern Siberia—neither more nor less.

Mr. Jujakoff, a distinguished press writer and publicist, son of a major-general and rich land-owner of the south of Russia, was exiled by Todleben to Eastern Siberia on the following grounds (textual): (1) because he belonged to a dangerous family, all the members of which (except the general) were imbued with perverse ideas. (His mother had been arrested and kept in prison for ten days for refusing to reveal the name of the owner of a socialist book ; his sister was in prison, and is now in Siberia.) (2) Because it was owing to his influence that certain leaders against the Socialists *were not printed* in the *Odessa Listok* after the attempt of April 2nd !

Mr. Kovalevsky, an officer of the Odessa municipality, was exiled to Eastern Siberia because (1) he was his wife's husband. (Madame Kovalevsky, while living at Kieff, away from her husband, became implicated in the Terrorist doings there, and was sentenced in May, 1879, to a term of hard labour.) (2) Because he had been heard to say, in presence of some of his fellow-officers of the municipality, that he had no very high opinion of the Government; and (3) because he exercised a bad influence over his friends.

The case of Mr. Belousoff, professor in one of the colleges at Kieff, is still richer. He was arrested in the summer of 1879, dismissed from his post and exiled to the north, all owing to a pure " misunderstanding," as they say in Russia, on the part of the police, and pure misfortune on his; the head and front of the poor man's offending being the name he bore—the name of Belousoff. So did somebody else with whom the police confounded him. Five years previously this somebody else had been accused, or suspected, of carrying on a propaganda among the workmen of Kieff, but succeeded in escaping. Thus Mr. Belousoff was made to suffer for the sins of a namesake whom he neither knew nor had ever seen. Already, in 1874, he had been brought before the police under a similar misapprehension, and the error being explained, dismissed—presumably "without a stain on his character." In 1879, however, he was less fortunate, for this time the police (who had doubtless on overhauling their records found his name thereon) condemned him to an indefinite term of administrative exile.

It may be remarked, by way of parenthesis, that this sort of *quid pro quo* is far from being uncommon in Russia. At Kharkoff a student named Semenovsky was arrested for no other reason than that, three years before, an advocate, similarly named, had been tried and convicted of propagandism. At Odessa, again, the police wanted a certain Mr. Kohan; but there being "two Richmonds in the field," they hesitated at first which to take, but got over the difficulty by arresting both.

But let us continue Mr. Belousoff's story. When the mistake was explained to General Tchertkoff, Governor of Kieff, and he was requested to revoke

the sentence passed on an admittedly innocent man,
he answered in these words : "I quite believe that
what you say is quite true; but in a time of trouble
like the present, the administration cannot afford to
make mistakes. So let him go into exile, and in a
little while he may petition me for a revocation !"

Another example in conclusion. Mr. Isidor Goldsmith was for eight years editor of two high-class
monthly reviews. When, in 1879, the rigours of the
censorship obliged him to abandon the career of
letters, he betook himself to Moscow, of which city
his wife (a member of the well-known Androusoff
family) was a native, and began practice at the bar.
But an untoward, yet all too common, incident
thwarted his plans, and involved himself and his
wife in interminable trouble. They were denounced
by a spy, who accused them to the police of having
come to Moscow for nothing else than to organize a
central revolutionary committee. Search and arrest
followed as a matter of course, and, equally of course,
nothing whatever was found to justify the statement
of the spy and the action of the police. All the same,
a formal inquisition was opened, and in ordinary circumstances the accused would have been kept in
prison during the six months over which an examination extended. But having friends in high quarters
and the absurdity of the charge against them being

self-evident, the Governor-General of Moscow, Prince Dolgorouky, was prevailed upon to interest himself in their favour. The consequence was that, instead of being locked up in gaol, they were placed under domiciliary arrest in their own house. But on September 24th they were arrested a second time, and without more ado sent under escort to Archangelsk, on the shores of the White Sea, the chief town of the province of that name. After a stay there of two months, they were transferred to the little town of Kholmogory in the same district. Before being conveyed to their new destination, Mr. Goldsmith had the good fortune to get sight of the document in which the grounds of the action taken against himself and his wife were set forth. It ran as follows :

"The gendarmery department of Moscow , accused Mr. Isidor Goldsmith and his wife Sophia of having come to Moscow intent on founding a central revolutionary committee. After a minute domiciliary search and an examination for the discovery of proofs, the charges brought against the before-mentioned persons were found to be quite without justification. Consequently the Minister of the Interior and the chief of the gendarmery decree that Isidor Goldsmith and Sophia his wife be transported to Archangelsk, and there placed under the supervision of the local police."

Could logic more exquisite be imagined ? These people are innocent, *therefore* let them be punished, a result so incredibly and grotesquely absurd that the uninitiated may well be excused for preferring to ascribe it rather to an error of transcription than to deliberate intention. But the reader, who is beginning to understand the spirit which animates the Tzar's bureaucracy, and has had time to familiarize himself with the manners and customs of official Russia, will find no difficulty in filling up the hiatus which seems to disconnect the syllogism from the conclusion in this remarkable and, unfortunately, by no means exceptional document.

The charge being false, says, in effect, the Third Section, there can be no ground for a formal prosecution. But as people who have once been accused are always looked upon with suspicion, this gentleman and his wife, in accordance with the usual custom in such cases, must be sent into exile.

And I repeat it, the cases I have adduced are neither exceptional nor extreme. The victims whose experiences we have narrated were able to ascertain, directly or indirectly, the causes to which their exile was ostensibly due. In every instance the cause was political. But there is ample room for the play of other and even darker causes; the methods of the police especially lending themselves to the gratification of private malice and personal revenge. For they not alone protect and support their own creatures —spies by profession—but do all in their power to encourage the spontaneous denunciations of amateur informers. An accused person is never, in any circumstances, allowed to know the name of his accuser, and the charge is always so worded as to throw you off the scent, and prevent you, as far as possible, from guessing the name of your secret enemy. For instance, the police will protest that they are in possession of evidence showing that you have distributed revolutionary proclamations; but where, when, or in what circumstances, they will no more tell you than they will divulge the name of their informant. It is, moreover, a positive fact that a great many persons ordered into exile are neither told the reason why, nor informed what they have done amiss. A few years later, perhaps, they may learn, by some indirect means, that they owe their ruin to a rogue whom they had threatened with prosecution, or a *chantagist* (I use the French word because there is no English equivalent) to whom they had refused black-mail. As I have already had occasion to mention, the Revising Commission appointed by Loris Melikoff discovered so many cases of exile arising from false evidence, that the Government itself was seized with horror. So at least the censured journals of the day emphatically affirmed. That the number of these cases was something enormous we can well believe. Under the existing system it would be surprising if they were not. But it may be permitted to doubt the sincerity of the horror ascribed to the Government. In any event it did not last long, and was speedily forgotten in the greater horror inspired by the dread spectre of revolution. For the system flourishes in full vigour even now, and in every city of the empire the best, the bravest, and the ablest continue to be torn from work profitable to themselves and useful to the country, and sent into hopeless exile.

But what, it may be asked, is this administrative exile ? We know that in ordinary parlance it means simple deportation. We know, too, what like is the supervision exercised by the police of continental countries over common criminals whose offences are considered not to have been sufficiently expiated by their previous punishment—an onerous and vexatious system that tends only to increase crime, and is strongly disapproved by the best authorities of the countries in which it prevails. But the Russian system of political exile is altogether *sui generis.* The person exiled is much more than a malefactor. The crime he is credited with a desire to commit is speech—the utterance of words. Worse than a malefactor, he is a centre of contagion. Because, when you come near a man he talks—and if his disposition be perverse and his political views unsound, he will inevitably poison with his venom all with whom he comes in contact—if you let him.

Hence he must be isolated, even in the place of his exile. Nor is this all. A man of culture can infect even at a distance. By means of letters and the Press he may corrupt people whom he never sees. It is therefore imperative to cut him off from the entire world.

And this is the principle acted upon, as the following extracts (textually rendered) from the Regulations for Administrative Exiles (March 12–25) will show:

"To exiles is forbidden:—Every sort of pedagogic occupation, such as the teaching of arts and trades, the reading (or giving) of public lectures, participation in the proceedings of scientific societies, and all public activity whatsoever!"

They are forbidden further to act as " typographers, lithographers, photographers, or librarians, or to serve in any such establishments as agents, clerks, over-lookers, or simple workmen." The vending of books, or other printed matter or product of the Press, is likewise forbidden to exiles (paragraph 24).

All other employments (?) not forbidden by the law (say, manual labour, for which the average political exile is little apt) are open to exiles, with the reservation, however, that the local governor may veto the occupation selected, in the event of the exile using it for the carrying out of perverse intentions, or if, owing to special circumstances, it is likely to endanger order or disturb the public tranquillity (paragraph 28).

By paragraph 21 it is forbidden to employ exiles in government offices or local public establishments, except as copyists, and by special permission of the Minister of the Interior. Paragraph 27 lays an interdict on medical or pharmaceutical practice by exiles, except, as in the former case, by special permission of the Minister. But as such permission is as hard to obtain as a revocation of the decree of exile, the interdict is practically absolute.

As the Government deprives exiles of almost every possible way of gaining a livelihood, it is only just that it should keep them. And this it does—after a fashion. In the central provinces they are allowed the pittance of six roubles (about sixteen shillings) a month; in the northern provinces, where life is more costly, the allowance is eight roubles—in both cases for exiles of the nobility. Members of the non-privileged classes receive exactly half this sum, and, as may be supposed, it is almost more than any of them can do to keep body and soul together.

And then comes paragraph 37, which reads like the bitterest irony: "Exiles who shirk work, either from idleness, bad conduct, or lazy habits, will be deprived of their governmental stipend!"

Finally, we have paragraph 29, which is, perhaps, the cream of the collection. It runs thus:

"The Minister of the Interior is empowered to

forbid to any exile the direct delivery of his letters
and despatches which, in that event, are to be handed
by the post-office to the chief of the local police or
the gendarmes. These latter, after reading them,
may give them to the exile, if they find nothing prejudicial therein. In the contrary case, the confiscated
correspondence must be immediately forwarded to the
gendarmery. In the same way all letters or dis-
patches which the exile proposes to send away must
be first read by the aforementioned authorities."

Practically, as we have good reasons to know, these
rules are applied in the inverse sense—all our exile's
correspondence is submitted to the censorship of the
local police. The contrary is the exception.

It is not difficult to picture to ourselves what life
must be like under conditions such as these. But as
an illustration, and by way of facilitating the process,
I will, with the reader's permission, tell the story of
a company of my exiled friends. Those who prefer to
trust to their own unaided imaginations are, of course,
at liberty to skip the following chapter. Let us, then,
leaving laws, regulations, and articles, deal for a moment
with creatures of flesh and blood, and study a deeply
interesting but little known phase of human life.

NEW BOOKS

AT ALL

LIBRARIES & BOOKSELLERS.

RUSSIA UNDER THE TZARS. By STEPNIAK, Author of "Underground Russia," etc. Translated by WILLIAM WESTALL. 2 vols. Crown 8vo. 18s.

THE NEW POLITICS: An Apology for the Life of Mr. Gladstone. Crown 8vo. 7s. 6d.

SONGS FROM THE NOVELISTS. Edited, and with Introduction and Notes, by W. DAVENPORT ADAMS. Foolscap 4to. Printed in coloured ink on handsome paper. Rough edges, gilt top. Bound in illuminated vellum.

COURT LIFE BELOW STAIRS; or, London Under the Four Georges. By J. FITZGERALD MOLLOY. 2 vols. Crown 8vo. 12s.

LEAVES FROM THE LIFE OF A SPECIAL CORRESPONDENT. By JOHN AUGUSTUS O'SHEA. 2 vols. Crown 8vo. 21s.

PHILOSOPHY IN THE KITCHEN. By the OLD BOHEMIAN. [*Shortly.*

WARD AND DOWNEY,

12, YORK STREET, COVENT GARDEN, LONDON.

THE NEW NOVELS.

THE FLOWER OF DOOM, and Other Stories.
By M. BETHAM-EDWARDS, Author of "Kitty," etc.
Crown 8vo. 6s. [*In June.*

A MAIDEN ALL FORLORN. By the Author
of "Phyllis," "Molly Bawn," etc. 3 vols. Crown 8vo.
31s. 6d.

MORNING GREY. By G. M., Author of "Ade,"
etc. 3 vols. 31s. 6d.

LIKE LOST SHEEP. By ARNOLD GRAY, Author
of "The Wild Warringtons," etc. 3 vols. 31s. 6d.

SOME STAINED PAGES. By the Author of
"The New Mistress," etc. 3 vols. Crown 8vo.
31s. 6d.

LIL LORIMER. By THEO GIFT, Author of "Pretty
Miss Bellew," etc. 3 vols. 31s. 6d.

THE PRETTIEST WOMAN IN WARSAW.
By MABEL COLLINS, Author of "Our Bohemia," etc.
3 vols. 31s. 6d.

NOT EVERY DAY: A Love Octave. By CON-
STANCE MacEWEN. 2 vols. Crown 8vo. 21s.

JOHN FORD. By FRANK BARRETT, Author of
"Folly Morrison," "Honest Davie," etc. 2 vols.
12s.

In Coloured Wrapper. Price 1s.
GEORGE MANVILLE FENN'S NEW NOVEL.

THE DARK HOUSE: A Knot Unravelled.

WARD AND DOWNEY,

12, YORK STREET, COVENT GARDEN, LONDON.

NEW EDITIONS OF POPULAR NOVELS.

By B. L. FARJEON.

GREAT PORTER SQUARE: A Mystery.
Fifth Edition. 6s.

THE HOUSE OF WHITE SHADOWS. 6s.

GRIF: A Story of Australian Life. 3s. 6d.

By RICHARD DOWLING.

THE DUKE'S SWEETHEART. Picture boards,
2s.; cloth, 2s. 6d.

UNDER ST. PAUL'S. Picture boards, 2s.; cloth,
2s. 6d.

THE SPORT OF FATE. Picture boards, 2s.;
cloth, 2s. 6d.
[In the Press.

By FRANK BARRETT.

FOLLY MORRISON. 3s. 6d.

HONEST DAVIE. Picture boards, 2s.; cloth,
2s. 6d.

By the Author of " Court Life Below Stairs."

IT IS NO WONDER. By J. FITZGERALD MOLLOY.
[In the Press.

By the Author of " Pretty Miss Neville."

PROPER PRIDE. By B. M. CROKER. 6s.

WARD AND DOWNEY,
12, YORK STREET, COVENT GARDEN, LONDON.